Gwendolen Trench Gascoigne

Among Pagodas and Fair Ladies

An account of a tour through Burma

Gwendolen Trench Gascoigne

Among Pagodas and Fair Ladies
An account of a tour through Burma

ISBN/EAN: 9783744755474

Printed in Europe, USA, Canada, Australia, Japan

Cover: Foto ©Andreas Hilbeck / pixelio.de

More available books at **www.hansebooks.com**

AMONG PAGODAS

AND

FAIR LADIES

AN ACCOUNT OF A TOUR THROUGH BURMA

BY

GWENDOLEN TRENCH GASCOIGNE

AUTHOR OF "A STEP ASIDE"

WITH NUMEROUS ILLUSTRATIONS

LONDON

A. D. INNES & CO.

BEDFORD STREET

1896

𝕴 Dedicate

THIS LITTLE BOOK TO

MR. DONALD SMEATON, C.S.I.

(Financial Commissioner for Burma),

IN MEMORY OF A DELIGHTFUL SOJOURN

IN THE COUNTRY THAT

HE LOVES.

PREFACE.

..

A SMALL portion of this little book first made
its appearance in the pages of *The Sporting
and Dramatic News*, and I am indebted to the
Editor of that journal for his courtesy in allowing me to use the articles. I wish also to express my gratitude to Mr. Donald Smeaton,
C.S.I. (Financial Commissioner for Burma), Mrs.
Manook, and Mr. Bridge (Deputy Commissioner
for Mandalay), for the kind assistance that they
rendered to me in giving me much valuable in-
formation. I beg also to tender my best thanks
to Messrs. Watson and Skeen, of Rangoon, and
Messrs. Beato and Johannes, of Mandalay, for
their valuable aid in allowing me to use their
excellent photographs.

NOTE.

— ..

THE author of these bright sketches succeeds in rendering her subjects attractive even to those who are already familiar with them; and this is a kind of success which is not often attained.

She came to Burma on a visit, and fell in love with the country and people at first sight. This accounts for the freshness and warmth of her colouring and her artist sympathy with the little things that concern the people. She has caught their quaint picturesque ways and pourtrayed them with fidelity. Text and pictures are true to life. I have enjoyed the little book, and so will all those who read it.

The land of rubies and pearls and gold—the home of a merry, kindly, laughing people—and destined at no very distant time to rule the commerce between Western and Eastern Asia—Burma claims the attentive and sympathetic study of our countrymen at home; and I recommend this little book to them for their introductory lesson.

DONALD SMEATON.

GOVERNMENT HOUSE, RANGOON.
July 20. 1896.

CONTENTS.

CHAP.   PAGE

 I. The Burmese and their Characteristics 19

 II. The Burmese Women   ... 43

 III. Pagodas   62

 IV. Miscellaneous ...   91

 V. Mandalay   119

 VI. Mandalay—The Palace ... 142

 VII. On the River   ... 168

 VIII. Bhamo and Tsembo   189

 IX. The Flora of Burma   ... 212

 X. On the River below Mandalay ... 224

 XI. Rice—and its Treatment ... 249

 XII. "Pohn-gyees" ...   262

 XIII. Burmese Language and Literature 277

 XIV. Ear-boring, Tattooing, and the Burial of
    the Dead   ... 294

LIST OF ILLUSTRATIONS.

..

SHWAY DAGOHN   *Frontispiece*

PAGE

THE QUAY AND MARKET, RANGOON   24

RANGOON   26

LITTLE BURMESE GIRLS DRESSED FOR A PWÉ   33

A BURMESE LADY ...   35

A BURMESE SCHOOL   39

A BURMESE BEAUTY   44

BURMESE GIRLS   ...   49

A BURMESE GIRL MAKING CHEROOTS ...   55

A BURMESE GIRL DRESSING HER HAIR   ...   58

A DANCING GIRL POSTURING ...   59

THE SHWAY DAGOHN   63

VIEW OF THE GOLDEN PAGODA FROM DALHOUSIE PARK ...   66

MONASTERIES AND REST - HOUSES ROUND THE GOLDEN
     PAGODA   68

SOUTHERN ENTRANCE TO THE GOLDEN PAGODA ...   70

PAGE

VIEW OF THE GOLDEN PAGODA FROM CANTONMENT GARDEN   75

SHRINES SURROUNDING THE GOLDEN PAGODA   ...   77

DOORWAY AT THE SUMMIT OF STEPS LEADING TO THE
    GOLDEN PAGODA   79

THE GREAT BELL AT THE GOLDEN PAGODA   ...   81

THE SULAY PAGODA...   85

ELEPHANTS AT WORK STACKING TIMBER   ...   92

ELEPHANT PUSHING A LOG INTO POSITION   93

DALHOUSIE PARK   ...   94

DRIVE BY THE SIDE OF THE LAKE IN DALHOUSIE PARK ...   95

THE LAKE, DALHOUSIE PARK   ...   99

A EUROPEAN BUNGALOW   ... 105

CARTS BEING LOADED WITH PINEAPPLES   108

A COUNTRY PWÈ   114

GIRLS DANCING AT A PWÈ   117

BIRD'S-EYE VIEW OF MANDALAY AND THE SEVEN HUNDRED
    AND SEVENTY-SEVEN PAGODAS   121

A BURMAN HOUSE   ...   126

A MANDALAY CART 129

AN UP-COUNTRY CART   133

BURMESE GIRLS WEAVING WITH A HAND-LOOM 136

THE PALACE, MANDALAY...   143

GARDEN ON SOUTHERN SIDE OF THE PALACE   146

A BURMESE SOLDIER IN KING THEBAW'S TIME   ...   149

PAGE

THE PALACE 151

THE MINISTER OF POLICE IN KING THEBAW'S TIME ... 158

PORTION OF THE INCOMPARABLE PAGODA ... 160

THE COWN MHE DAW ... 164

THE QUEEN'S MONASTERY AT MANDALAY 166

MINGOHN PAGODA 169

THE GREAT BELL 171

A TEAK RAFT 177

A NATIVE VILLAGE 183

ENTRANCE TO SECOND DEFILE 187

BHAMO 190

THE CHINESE QUARTER OF BHAMO 193

SHAN MAN AND WOMAN 197

THE FIRST DEFILE ... 200

NEAR THE ELEPHANT ROCK. FIRST DEFILE ... 201

NEAR THE PASHA GATE. FIRST DEFILE 203

TSEMBO 209

TEAK RAFTS ... 219

NATIVE VILLAGE BELOW MANDALAY ... 227

AN IRRAWADDY SAILING BOAT ... 229

PAGAHN 231

PAGAHN 235

PROME 239

18   LIST OF ILLUSTRATIONS.

	PAGE
NATIVE BOATS, RANGOON... ...	255
POHN-GYEES TEACHING ...	... 263
A BEGGING MONK	268
THE PYRE	... 273
A POHN-GYEE BYAN	275
SHIPPING AT RANGOON	... 310

CHAPTER I.

OUT of the infinite variety of travellers who visit the East, comparatively few stay their steps, or turn aside in their wanderings, to look upon Burma.

To many, Burma is a mere name on the map: a place where some ten years ago we deposed a king named Thebaw and annexed a further large tract of country which was at that time full of Dacoits, fever, and rubies; the last named can be purchased now with greater ease at Mr. Streeter's, in Bond Street!

Therefore, until lately, Burma has been left in comparative peace, and has been spared that most terrible of all scourges, the globe-trotter. True, a few of the most inveterate Yankees have journeyed every winter up the Irrawaddy, done Rangoon and Mandalay, asked questions, criticised everything, and at the end have come to the satisfactory conclusion that there exists no country and no people

19

but the Americans. I doubt myself if those same
contented Yankees did really see Burma; of course,
in American parlance, they "did it," but Burma
and the Burmese require something more subtle
than a mere casual hurried glance. They want a
steadfast concentrated gaze beneath the surface, a
little microscopic inspection, a little old-world
leisure to enable you to obtain any real insight
into their ways, habits, legends, and character.

The idea of paying a visit to Burma presented
itself to us like one of those happy chances that
do occasionally fall to people's lot, and it is a
chance for which we shall always be grateful.
We left England with no more idea of going to
Burma than we had of going to the moon! We
merely intended to make the usual respectable,
stereotype Indian tour, when fortune (that fickle
muse) decreed that among the many pleasant
fellow-passengers on board that most excellent
ship the *Oriental*, we should have the good fortune
to make the acquaintance of Mr. Donald Smeaton,
Financial Commissioner for Burma. Few people
have the knowledge and interest in Burma that
Mr. Smeaton possesses, and few people have had
his enormous energy in carrying out and develop-
ing the country under his charge in the way that
he has done. Mr. Smeaton has an intense love
for Burma and its inhabitants, and the many years
which he has spent there, both before and after

the annexation, have given him an insight and sympathy with his surroundings which is rarely found, and ought indeed to be rarely prized. It was owing to Mr. Smeaton's advice, and to his warm and hospitable invitation to stay with him and Mrs. Smeaton at Rangoon, that we decided to give up a part of our tour in Northern India, and instead direct our steps to Burma ; and it was in consequence of this decision that in the middle of February, 1895, we found ourselves steaming down to Diamond Harbour to join the British India steamer *Africa*, which was to bear us to Rangoon. We were spared the voyage down the Hooghly, as the mails arrived late that week, and were therefore sent on to Diamond Harbour by train to join the ship. I was not inconsolable at thus missing that portion of the journey, as I confess to having a holy horror of the Hooghly and its horrible erie currents and terrible James and Mary sandbanks, where so many a good ship has gone down. The pilot arrangements are marvellous, and the survey of the river most complete. As these sandbanks are constantly shifting, a system of telegraph is in practice to give notice of the exact position of these sandbanks, but even with that assistance the difficulty and danger of navigation is enormous. The Hooghly pilots are too well known to fame to need any words of mine in their praise. We carried ours, a very pleasant young man, with us to Ran-

goon, and at the mouth of the Irrawaddy we took
another one on board to take the ship up the Irrawaddy, which is also, though in a far less degree,
very difficult of navigation. In any case we felt
extremely well protected with two pilots and a
captain on board.

The journey from Calcutta to Rangoon takes
from three to four days, and in the winter is not
unpleasant, even though it has to be accomplished
in a British India steamer, where cockroaches are
too frequent guests, the cooking not quite on a par
with the Café Anglais, and where the deck room
reserved for the European passengers is of a very
limited description.

Our voyage was splendid. We floated easily
and happily over a summer sea, upon which no
ripple came to disturb our tranquillity.

Our first view of Burma was a low uneven coast,
showing over our port quarter, and at the same
time we noticed, though then miles from the land,
that the whole sea much resembled the colour of
pea-soup, a dark, muddy brown, and the water was
absolutely thick with the particles of sand. This
sand is swept down from the many mouths of the
Irrawaddy, which flow into the Bay of Bengal at
that point.

The country that you look upon after entering
the river on the way up to Rangoon is flat, and
possesses no very striking feature of interest. As

THE QUAY AND MARKET, RANGOON.

you approach nearer to the town, your gaze lights
upon innumerable rice mills of every grade, large
and small. These mills have increased immensely
during recent years, and Rangoon is now one of
the largest depôts for rice, and the amount tran-
shipped from there every year is something fabu-
lous. The rice-mills cannot be accused of being
in the least ornamental, their horrible smoking
chimneys remind one very unpleasantly of Bir-
mingham, Sheffield, or Leeds. The country is not
prepossessing, and the river, though broad, is of
the same dirty brown hue, and like the sea, thick
with sand. Everything at this point is ugly and
unattractive with the one blessed exception, "the
great Golden Pagoda," which shines forth from its
green hill sparkling and exulting in its own splendid
magnificence, and giving one a thrill of joy and
delight as one's eyes rest upon it. It seems
from the river to tower above Rangoon, to stand
there like a brilliant golden sentinel guarding the
inhabitants from evil. At first it is a mere glittering speck among the green verdure, but at each
bend of the river it grows, and grows, until at
length the graceful proportions are fully revealed,
and the airy spire is distinctly visible its delicate
point stretching far up towards the blue heavens.

On approaching near to Rangoon the river was
crowded with shipping, it being part of the busiest
season of the year when the rice is being packed

and despatched to all parts of the world. Every
kind and condition of ship were lying off to bear
the much coveted grain away. Besides the rice-
boats there were endless craft from every part of
the world. Great passenger steamers of the Bibi
Line, British India steamers, Irrawaddy river
steamers, not to mention sampans and dugouts

RANGOON.

which flew about in all directions. The scene on
the quay was a most animated one, and the colour,
noise, and general picturesqueness made it one of
great interest and attractiveness.

My first impression of Rangoon was one of un-
mitigated delight. I expected to land in a country
much resembling India, and instead I discovered
that I was in a new world, and one that was in

many respects infinitely more picturesque, and
possessed even more charm and originality.

Rangoon itself is a large flourishing town with a
population of some 180,324. It is the centre of
the government and official administrations of
Burma, and besides possesses an enormous commercial colony. The actual town is decidedly
attractive ; the streets are broad, many of the
public buildings are fine, and the infinite variety
of architecture of which the houses are composed
gives it a very distinct and unique character. In
one street you may see European, Burmese, and
Chinese houses side by side, and bearing each
other company in excellent part, the picturesqueness of the two latter throwing a kindly halo of
beauty over their less comely and more commonplace neighbour.

The inhabitants of Rangoon have quite as much
variety as the architecture of their houses. The
native of India is to be seen squatting in any
conveniently shady corner. John Chinaman, with
his long pig-tail and broad, good-tempered countenance, stalks along as if the whole place belonged
to him ; the Burra-Memsaib with her smart pony-
cart, and a husband who receives his thousand
rupees a month, dashes in and out among the
motley crowd ; and last, but oh ! not least, the
Burmese themselves, with their charming personality, their brilliant coloured dresses, and their

easy, joyous light-heartedness, flit about, or stand
in picturesque groups holding gay and animated
converse.

The Burmese have been called the " Irish of the
East," I should rather designate them as " the
Italians of the East." They possess that peculiar
charm of being intensely *simpatica*, which is so
distinct an attribute of the Italian race. The
courteous manners, the delight in mere existence,
the childish pleasure of the moment and the
intense love of a joke—though perhaps this latter
is more Irish than Italian—all these delightful
qualities are theirs, and certainly their sense of
humour is the most acute that I have ever beheld.
It is said that if a Burman's house takes fire he
laughs instead of cries, and then gets up a Pwè
(native play) on the charred ruins. I remember
being much struck with this same sense of humour
at Mandalay. When we were embarking upon the
steamer, a crowd of about twenty youths gathered
round to take our four or five little boxes on to the
boat. My husband, who had become rather tired
of paying twenty people where four would do, told
our native bearer to choose three or four out of the
crowd and send off the rest. This, however, was
not so easily manœuvred, and words had to be
a little emphasised with fists, which resulted in
some of the gay Burmans taking a slight roll in
their native sand, but this did not in the least

disconcert or anger them. They merely looked
upon it as a most excellent joke, and peals of
laughter were the only result. The Burman, alas!
resembles the Italian in some of his bad qualities;
in his love of idleness he is essentially given to a
dolce far niente existence, or let us say that he is
extremely successful in his power of doing nothing.
He is generous to an amazing degree; the hoard-
ing of money which is so strong a characteristic of
the native of India does not seem to be a part of
the Burman's nature. If a Burman is possessed
of a little money it is generally expended upon
what is described as a work of merit. The building of a pagoda, the making a road, or the con-
structing of a bridge, all of which works are
supposed to bring great *kudos* in this world, and
a rich reward in the next. Should his money not
be expended in this laudable manner it is probably
spent on a Pwè (native play), or in gambling or
betting. The Burman again resembles the Italian
in his inveterate love of games of chance; he is
the most confirmed gambler that it is possible to
imagine. A horse race, a cock fight, a boat race,
or cards, have the most curious fascination for
him, and his excitement on the two former occasions is absolutely grotesque. As the horses come
by, or the boats flash past, he dances, shrieks,
laughs, pulls his hair down, takes his coat off, in
fact, behaves like the child that he is. In no way,

perhaps, can one better describe the incongruity of
his nature than by saying that he is nothing more
than a charming child: with all the delightful
freshness of youth, the absolute abandonment
of himself to the present moment, without any
gnawing anxiety for the future—that future which
in his undevelopment he perhaps does not entirely
realise. He again resembles the Italian in his
curiously superstitious nature. The Burman's
fear of the evil eye and of evil spirits which they
call "Nats," is prodigious. Their belief in witch-
craft, and in the importance of lucky days, new
moons, the efficacy of charms of all sorts, &c., are
among their most steadfast beliefs.

In religion they are Buddhists, but their intense
dread of demons and nats, which they are always
striving to propitiate, amounts almost to a second
religion, and one which, in many cases, produces
a stronger hold upon them. The Burman is
innately courteous and given to hospitality; not
that he has quite arrived at that generous pitch
which is now so much in vogue with certain
fashionable London dames, of giving a magnificent entertainment to *other people's friends !* The
Burman wisely prefers to entertain his own friends,
and he is probably more fortunate than many a
London hostess, seeing that he possesses many of
them. We had a charming example of Burman
hospitality and courtesy while staying at Bhamo.

One morning as we were walking up the picturesque straggling street we passed a particularly attractive Burman house, with two charming little Burmese maidens seated in the verandah. I begged the friend with whom we were walking, and who spoke Burmese, if he would ask the little ladies if I might be allowed to see their home. They assented joyfully, and showed us all over with evident pride and satisfaction, and then gave me the warmest invitation to go and stay with them, adding that they would then show me all over Bhamo. I was, alas! reluctantly obliged to refuse this tempting offer, as we were leaving for Tsembo early the following morning.

Another example of courtesy was shown to us also at Bhamo. We were standing in the street one afternoon, watching a Pwè which was being acted, and we had not been there many minutes before two chairs were brought out and placed in a good position, and by signs we were made to understand that they were intended for us. After seating ourselves great care was taken that none of the audience should stand in front of us, or in any way impede our view of the proceedings.

I shall give a description of these Pwès later on, as they are a national institution, and a great feature of Burma.

Contentment is another strong characteristic of the Burmese. They do not resemble us of the restless West, who are for ever striving after something new, something that we do not possess. Life is easy in Burma ; the curse of Cain does not appear to have fallen upon this happy people, for the rice grows in glorious plenitude without the need of incessant toil. If a Burman has enough of that valuable product to eat, a smart " pasoh " (silk petticoat) to wear, sufficient cheroots to smoke, betel-nut to chew, and a little money to gamble with, he is quite content.

No doubt this lack of ambition is in many ways very derogatory to the progress of the country. The Burman's apathy and dislike to any work has unfortunately made it absolutely necessary to import much foreign labour, and now nearly all the work of the country is done by coolies from India and Chinamen. This influx from India and China is, alas! much on the increase, and is greatly to be deplored, as it is feared that by degrees the Burmans as a distinct race will disappear altogether, or become so merged into the other races that they will lose all their individuality and distinct characteristics.

In personal appearance the Burmese are very small, their type of features being decidedly Japanese, from their Mongolian descent. Their faces are broad and flat, and the eyes inclined to be almond-shaped, and placed rather far apart. In complexion they are light coloured. Some of the girls are excessively pretty, and the dress of both sexes is most picturesque. The woman's costume consists of a loose white linen jacket, or should they be rich, of a brocaded jacket, with rather large bell-shaped sleeves, and a " tamehn " which is a long piece of silk or cotton, about a yard and a half in length and a trifle less in width.

LITTLE BURMESE GIRLS DRESSED FOR A PWÈ.

This " tamehn " is generally made in two pieces, of different patterns, the lower part forming a border. The " tamehn " is worn like a very tight skirt, and is fastened round the chest, the two ends being attached together by a wonderfully cunning twist which, astonishing as it may seem, appears to make the garment quite secure. This petticoat displays clearly the symmetry of the figure that it covers, and, unless managed with great dexterity, and worn by a person who is fully versed in the swaying movement necessary to keep it in its place, might possibly leave a trifle less than was desirable to the imagination! Over their shoulders they throw a dainty little coloured shawl, or, if they are very smart, a fine piece of embroidered crêpe. Their hair is black, and generally long and silky, and this they wear coiled round and round on the crown of the head in what is called a "sadohn," on one side of which they arrange with much taste a bunch of flowers. Should nature not have been bountiful to them in the matter of hair, they add on false tails freely without the smallest shame, and you see the men as well as the women washing their false tails and putting them on with the most amusing *sang froid!* The colouring of the silks and the coquettish manner in which a Burmese woman dresses herself, makes her a most attractive and picturesque vision.

The men's dress bears a strong resemblance to that of the women, and is quite as fascinating in its way. They wear the same kind of large white linen jacket, and a shorter silk petticoat called a " pasoh "; this is a straight piece of stuff generally of some delicate soft-hued silk measuring about seven to eight yards long, and one yard broad. This petticoat has no border, and is consequently much

shorter than the women's "tamehn," and displays
a good portion of calf and ankle, but what it loses
in length it more than gains in width, as it is

A BURMESE LADY.

most voluminous in its proportions. This garment is worn in much the same manner as the
"tamehn" except that it is bound round the loins

instead of round the chest. It is attached with
the same cunning twist of the ends and it then
hangs down in front in flowing, graceful folds,
rather resembling a large sash. The men wear
their hair long and are extremely proud of having
as much as they can, false or real! They wear it
also coiled, but put on the very top of the head in
what they designate by the term "young"; round
this they tie turban-fashion a brilliant coloured
handkerchief, the ends of which hang tastefully
down on one side. It is a wonderfully becoming
dress, and a group of Burmans is quite one of
the most pleasing and picturesque sights imaginable.

Another of their most cherished pleasures, which
might be termed a strong characteristic or habit,
as it is most prevalent among all the Burmese, is
their extraordinary devotion to smoking. Men,
women, and even children—I have seen tiny
things of not more than four or five puffing away
with evident satisfaction and delight at enormous
cigars. The Burmese cheroots are prodigious in
size, measuring from ten to twelve inches long,
and about three-quarters of an inch in diameter,
but they are, I am told, very mild. The women
manage their smoking with astonishing grace, and
there is a coquettish charm in the way that they
wield their gigantic cheroots, and a delightful
pucker of their rosebud mouths as they try to

grasp them with their little red lips, which adds to rather than detracts from their charms.

There is no denying that the Burman is a volatile, changeable creature. This characteristic even displays itself in the children, who, I am told, often become weary of one school and go to another, and then tire of that and try a third, and so on, merely for the pleasure of change.

The Burman is, I fear, also hardly a trustworthy individual; not the least from any evil-mindedness, but merely that with his airy, *légère* character he forgets; or at the moment that a duty has to be performed it is not a lucky time to do it, and so it does not commend itself to him, and he therefore calmly ignores the whole thing. For instance, I am told that a Burman is seldom or never employed as a signalman, for the excellent reason that he would one day turn the signals on the right way, the next he would probably have forgotten all about the existence of such a thing as a train, or would have gone off to a Pwè or a pagoda feast, or perhaps it would not have been a lucky moment to do it in, so that the passengers and the train would have fared rather indifferently. And yet with all their faults and all their shortcomings there is no denying that, as a nation, they are a most fascinating people. One of the strongest impressions that you have with regard to a Burman, is that he is emphatically a " gentleman"; he has none of the cringing, whining, detestable manner of the native of India, and he possesses that essence of good breeding, of always being perfectly at his ease. Burma is a very democratic country, as there is no hereditary upper class.

Burmans are said to have an inordinately good opinion of themselves, and of their own capabilities. They put a high estimate on their own qualities, and no doubt they are not entirely unwise, for the world generally takes you at your own valuation; and if you have the opportunity of impressing sufficiently upon people that you are very clever or very smart, or very important, they generally, in time, end by believing you.

The Burmans are extremely fond of all sorts of games; they play a kind of chess in which they greatly delight, and boxing and football are both pastimes which appear much to commend themselves to them. Football they play with a vast deal of dexterity, tucking up their silk petticoats in a very amusing manner, and kicking the ball far into the air. It is quite a different game to our football. The players arrange themselves in a circle; they then start a very light, wicker-made ball, and the great object is to keep the ball going as long as possible, and not to allow it to fall to the ground. They are not allowed to touch the ball with the hand, but they catch it on

their shoulders, ankles, feet, &c., and they do
this with marvellous skill, sometimes even jump-
ing into the air and catching the ball on the heel.

It cannot be said that courage is a very strong
feature of the Burmese character. Fighting does
not form part of the things which their soul
generally hankers after. They are peaceably

A BURMESE SCHOOL.

inclined, and if they desire to obtain any especial
object they prefer that it should be gained by
craftiness rather than by force. An amusing story
of their diplomacy is told by Shway Yoe (Mr.
Scott) in his delightful book, which I venture
to quote : "The Burmans and the Shans (a
tribe who inhabits a large district of Upper
Burma) had a dispute over a fine tract of paddy

land. The Shans were perfectly ready to settle the question by force—not so the Burmans; that mode of procedure did not appeal to them, and they therefore resorted to diplomacy, and advised that the settlement of the question should be referred to the arbitration of an aged hermit, who suggested that the tribe who should first erect a pagoda should possess the much coveted land. Both sides accordingly set to work, but the Burmans soon discovered that the steady, hard-working Shans were entirely outstripping them. So they took counsel together, and determined to have recourse to stratagem, and at night they constructed a framework of bamboo, the required height of the proposed pagoda, they then draped the skeleton with cloth, which they covered with white plaster. The effect from a distance was so admirable that it completely deceived the Shans, who departed to their own country in despair, firmly impressed with the idea that a miracle had been performed."

There is rather a curious and interesting account given of the first authentic travellers in Burma by Sir Arthur Phayre in his history of Burma, which I also venture to quote in his own words:—

"The first authentic narrative of travel in the countries of the Irawadi is by a Venetian, Nicolò di Conti. This traveller resided during the first quarter of the fifteenth century at Damascus as a merchant. He proceeded to Bussorah, and thence by sea, in company with some Persian merchants, to Cambay and Ceylon. He next went to the port of Tenasserim, then a place of importance, and from that to Bengal. After having sailed up the river Ganges he returned to the coast, and took ship apparently at a port on the Megna for Arakan. He arrived at the estuary or mouth of the river, which he calls Racha, and which foreigners still call the Arakan river, though that is not the native name. He proceeded to the capital, which he correctly states has the same name as the river. He then went eastwards across the mountains, still apparently accompanied by some of his Persian friends until they reached the river Irawadi, which he calls Dava, no doubt from the name of the capital. He proceeded up to Ava, where he arrived probably during or about A.D. 1430, when Monhyin Mengtarâ was king. He names the country Macinus or Mahâchin, a term he learnt from his Persian or Indian companions. He describes two methods of trapping and taming wild elephants as practised by the natives, the white elephant kept by the king, the rhinoceros, and other animals. He mentions some customs characteristic of the people.

" Nicolò returned to the sea-coast by the Taungu routes, and speaks of the city of Pegu, the capital of the province of the same name.

"The next traveller, whose narrative of a visit
to Burma or Pegu has been preserved, is Athanasius
Nikitin of Iwer. He travelled in Asia between
the years 1468 and 1474. He went to the city of
Pegu, but only mentions the Indian traders there.
He does not note the difference of race between
them and the Burmese or Talaings.

"The Genoese merchant Hieronimo di Santo
Stefano went to India from Egypt with Hieronimo
Adorno from Coromandel; they came to Pegu, and
arrived at the city of that name in the year 1496.
This was during the reign of Binya Rân, King of
Pegu. He mentions Ava, where grow rubies and
many other precious stones. 'Our wish was to
go to this place, but at that time the two princes
were at war, so that no one was allowed to go from
the one place to the other.' The native histories
do not mention any actual war between the kings
of Pegu and Burma at this time; but Binya Rân
attacked Dwârawati, a city or fort belonging to
Taungu, which was very likely to bring about war
with Ava. Hieronimo Adorno died in Pegu on
St. John's Day. The property of the deceased
was seized as a forfeit to the king, according to the
law of Burma and Pegu in the case of foreigners
dying in the country. The property was, after
much delay, restored to the survivor, but the
traveller was detained in the country for a year
and a half."

CHAPTER II.

THE Burmese women are such an important and unique feature of Burma that I feel that they demand, ay, and deserve, a chapter to themselves. In no country, I think I may say—except perhaps in America—have women such a prominent position as in Burma. Utterly unlike their miserable Mahomedan and Hindoo sisters, they enjoy absolute liberty—a liberty of which, if rumour prove true, they make ample use.

Women's rights are not in Burma an illusive dream, a thing to be shrieked and struggled after, they are an accomplished fact.

The Burmese are all "new women," and take a very forward and active part in all matters pertaining to business. Few husbands would dare to enter into any mercantile arrangements without the aid or advice of their wives; at least the probability is that should any poor deluded man be so unwise he would hear a good deal more about the matter than he quite desired.

A Burmese woman is generally supposed to have quite as good a head for business, if not better, than her husband, and she is extremely clever in arranging a good bargain, and will often in her husband's absence drive a harder one than he would, and conduct the sale of a whole crop of paddy with masterly capability.

A BURMESE BEAUTY.

In matters pertaining to law, or with regard to property where legal documents have to be drawn up, and also in the case of taxes, the woman's name always appears as well as the man's; but there is another reason to be assigned for this, *i.e.*, that the Burmese have no surnames, so that the woman's name is partly introduced to avoid any mistake or confusion.

In that most important relation of life, marriage, the Burmese young lady practically settles the question for herself. She probably enjoys a good deal more liberty in her choice of a husband than is accorded to many an English maiden, though the latter certainly has the chance now of pursuing her victims on a bicycle, or let us say of being pursued by them!

The Burmese girl, though not yet possessed of that useful and excellent machine, is not slow to discover numerous places and opportunities for meeting her admirers. For instance, at the many pagoda feasts, at a Pwè, or when she goes marketing at the bazaar; all these are excellent rendezvous, and certainly, to judge from my own observations, she is not behindhand in the old-world art of flirtation. There is nothing vulgar in the way that she practises it. All is conducted with the utmost charm and grace, and the young man must be stony-hearted indeed if he does not fall down before the blandishments of one of these bewitching little damsels. As a matter of form, it is necessary that the girl should have her parents' consent to her marriage, as should she be unwise enough to marry without it they retain the power (should they choose to be so extremely disagreeable) of separating their daughter from her husband, even in the event of their having been married for some years and possessing children.

The parents' consent practically legalises the marriage.

Runaway matches are not unknown in Burma, but in such cases the parents are seldom very severe to the delinquents. They are too easy-going and too indolent to exert themselves to take any very strenuous measures, though occasionally in Lower Burma the father of the girl insists upon the separation of the young couple until the husband has procured a situation. But even this laudable and praiseworthy idea is usually abandoned, from the intense apathy and idleness of their natures, and the young people are simply blessed and forgiven.

After marriage it was formerly the custom for the bride and bridegroom to take up their abode (at all events for a time) with the bride's parents ; the girl was then able to learn from her mother the mysteries of becoming a good *Haus Frau*, while the fortunate husband was supposed to do his share of the work, to be at his dear mother-in-law's beck and call, and to help to sustain the home and make himself generally useful and agreeable. Charming and enviable position, no doubt, but not one, methinks, that would quite commend itself to an English husband !

However, such was the custom of the country, and very little choice was given to the young people, as should they have ventured to have put

forth new ideas, or advanced the unseemly sugges-
tion of setting up house alone they would have
been looked upon with great disfavour. With old-
fashioned people this custom is still continued.
Should the bride or bridegroom be an only child, the
couple remained with the parents until their death.
A very tender and filial action, and one much to
be commended, but it might perchance prove a
little trying and irksome to English tempers. The
Burmese are more amiable and more easy-going,
and they are also more ready to share the goods
which the gods have bestowed upon them, and are
not so grasping and avaricious. These customs, I
am told now, are no longer practised as a regular
thing.

It is permitted for a man to have two or more
wives should he desire it, but this is a custom
little in vogue in Burma, probably because the
Burman finds that one wife is generally more than
sufficient for him to manage, and that his life
would be one of great unrest, and become a
bewildering tangle of excitement if he possessed
more than one of these resolute but bewitching
little dames. I can well believe that a henpecked
husband is not quite an unknown quantity in
Burma.

The age at which most of the men marry is from
eighteen to twenty, and the girls from about four-
teen to fifteen. The preliminary love-making is

conducted in much the same manner as in other countries. The old, old story is related with the same fervour and devotion, and the little Burmese girls receive the tidings with charming flashes of their bright dancing brown eyes, and coquettish shrugs of their graceful little shoulders. The authorised courting, by which I mean the courting which takes place after the suitor has paid his addresses to the parents, and been approved by them, is carried on in a different and rather original manner.

It seldom takes place in daylight, the proper courting hour being between nine and ten o'clock at night, when a lamp is placed in the window by the young lady to give notice that she is ready to receive her admirer. The reason for this curious hour having been selected is hard to explain; it may be because the Burman is so indolent that he prefers to doze comfortably during the hot hours of the day, or that he vainly hopes to find his lady's heart kinder when the evening shadows lie on the tired earth, or when the moonbeams weave cunning webs of light around the sacred pagoda. Whatever the reason be, between nine and ten o'clock is the mystic hour, and at nine o'clock the young lover sallies forth to see " his fair lady."

He is attended by two or three chosen swains, and this gay company betake themselves to the bride's abode. Arrived at the house, they wait without

until they are informed that the parents have safely
disposed of themselves in bed. They are then
bidden to enter, and find the girl ready waiting to

BURMESE GIRLS.

receive the attentions of her lover. She is arrayed
in all her very best apparel, which probably consists of a delicate rose-pink "tamehn," with the

4

purest of white linen jackets. A dainty bunch of
flowers peeps wistfully out from among the dark,
glossy coils of her hair, while, if she be fairly well
to do, glistening gems glitter in her little ears, and
a fascinating embroidered crape scarf is thrown
across her shapely shoulders. If fair to see (and
we will imagine that she is so), she looks bewilder-
ingly charming with her flashing brown eyes, and
rosebud mouth drawn up into a becoming pout by
the prodigious cheroot at which she puffs with
intense satisfaction. The girl is sometimes alone,
sometimes also attended by a *chère amie*. When
this latter is the case, the two sets of friends are
probably not loth to entertain each other, and the
happy pair are left to undisputed enjoyment of
their blissful lovers' hour. The parents, though
supposed to be comfortably installed in bed and
asleep, are in reality very much awake, and are
keeping a silent but strict watch upon the proceedings of the young people, and they are quite
ready to check severely any courting on the part
of the lover which they consider a little too ardent
or demonstrative.

At length, when all the preliminary part has
been successfully accomplished, all the arrangements concluded, a proper dowry fixed upon, and
that most important of all important things in a
Burman's mind, a lucky day chosen, the marriage
takes place in the bride's house.

There is nothing whatever pertaining to a religious service about it, as Buddhists, to which faith the Burmese belong, do not consider that religion plays any part in what is to them a merely social contract, and a Buddhist priest would consider his presence at a wedding most out of place.

There is always a large feast, and of course a Pwè (native play), as a Burman can do nothing without that national amusement.

The only approach to a ceremony that does occasionally take place is the following : the bride and bridegroom are seated upon the ground opposite to each other, they are then bound together with a white scarf, and they eat a little rice out of the same bowl, and join their right hands together palm to palm. But even these extremely simple rites are more often dispensed with, and the feasting and the Pwè are considered amply sufficient to solemnise the union.

In some parts of Burma, in out-of-the-way country villages, they still retain a curious custom of tying a cord across the road along which the bridegroom must pass on his way to his home. They then demand money from him before he is allowed to proceed on his way. Should he refuse this backshish, they break the cord with a curse on the newly-married pair.

They have yet an older and still more disagreeable custom, which is, that on the wedding night a party of gay young bachelors assemble round the house of the newly-married pair, and pelt it with stones and sticks, which is extremely detrimental to the flimsy bamboo structures, and often results in serious damage being effected to the house, and not unfrequently to the occupants. This custom is especially curious, as it resembles a practice still occasionally in vogue in very out-of-the-way and rural villages in England, of throwing stones and firing guns round the abode of a newly-wedded pair.

Divorce is delightfully easy of attainment in Burma. Sir George Lewis and Sir Charles Russell would find their services little in requisition. The marriage ties are easily loosed and cast aside, almost for the mere asking.

A woman can leave her husband if he is poor and cannot support her, or if he leads a lazy life, or if he is old and ailing, or should become crippled after marriage, he can be readily disposed of! A man is at liberty to divorce his wife if she fail in presenting him with a male child; but I am not in a position to say what period of time the lady is allowed to fulfil her part of the compact; he can also divorce her if she does not show him proper affection, or if she persists in going to places of which he does not approve.

Temporary divorces are also occasionally resorted

to. A Burman told my friend Mr. Smeaton one
day, that he had not been quite satisfied with his
wife's behaviour, and that therefore he thought
that a temporary divorce would be a most ju-
dicious measure. I did not happen to hear if
the ladies also resort to this means with re-
fractory husbands, but I can quite believe that
it would be possible.

Probably because divorce is so easy of attainment it is not very frequently taken advantage of.
Burmans are very affectionate husbands and
fathers; family affection is a very strong trait of
the Burman character, and in the event of their
wives not always giving them complete satisfaction, they are generally too indolent, or let us
say too good-natured, to do more than reason with
them. When a Burmese woman marries, any
property which she may possess, either from her
own earnings or by inheritance, is hers entirely,
and is set apart for her children or heirs; and in
the event of her being divorced she has the power
of taking her own property away with her; also any
money that a wife earns herself after marriage
belongs exclusively to herself. Thus the Burmese
are quite as advanced and up to date, if not more
so, than we of the West, and I believe I am right
in saying that these laws concerning women's
property existed in Burma long before the Woman's
Property Act was passed in England.

The Burmese women put all their fortunes as a rule into jewellery. Some possess really lovely diamonds.

While staying with Mr. Donald Smeaton at Rangoon, many charming little Burmese ladies used to come to pay their *devoir* to Mrs. Smeaton. They would all come in and arrange themselves on the floor in a row, or in a circle, and laugh and chatter together like little birds, or if they brought an interpreter with them, they sat quiet with wistful little faces trying hard to understand what was said. Many of them, though not at all rich, had beautiful jewels, earrings and rings were what they mostly affected. The former were large rounds, set with five or six huge diamonds, emeralds, or rubies, which I noticed were always cut into sharp points, and not like ours in flat angles.

The earrings are all of the same pattern, and they showed us how cunningly devised they were, as the gold settings with the stones were made to unscrew and allow of other stones being substituted.

The little ladies took immense interest in our European clothes, and fingered them all over with profound wonder. I expect that in their hearts they thought them very ugly after their lovely silks.

The refreshments that they most delighted to partake of were jam, cake, and tea ; but the former was their great delight, and they ate it with enormous gusto, and generally with their fingers.

I met two or three Burmese ladies at Rangoon who were most charming, and spoke English extremely well. One of them was kind enough to go shopping with us one morning, and assisted us in bargaining for the lovely Burmese silks which are a great product

A BURMESE GIRL MAKING CHEROOTS.

of Burma. They are woven on hand looms, mostly at Mandalay and at Amarapura, and are of the most brilliant and yet with all the most artistic colours imaginable. The little shop to which we went would have made a charming study for an artist. The costly silks strewn about in a wondrous mass of warm glowing colour. In one

corner sat a group of Burmans choosing with
infinite care some new pasohs, fingering the
delicate materials with knowledgeable acuteness,
gossiping, smoking, and bargaining in their
indolent graceful way; while in the opposite
corner, we stood watching two or three dainty
Burmese maidens, who flitted here and there
dragging out each moment more of their tempting wares, and casting dazzling pieces of fabric
down before our eager gaze. We spent a delightful half hour in that seductive shop, but we came
out very much poorer than we went in.

I have said at the beginning of this chapter that
the Burmese are modern women, and so they
are in their capability, intelligence, business-like
habits and liberty; but how vastly different to the
modern woman of England; ay, at the risk of
their wishing to tear me in pieces, I must say it,
how enormously superior to the shrieking, lectur-
ing, struggling, unmannerly female, this terrible
product of the nineteenth century, who is for ever
screaming her rights upon platforms, and losing
all that delicate womanly charm, in which if she
could only be persuaded to see it, lies the secret
of her greatest influence. The Burmese woman
has shown herself far wiser: she has placed the
limitation at the right point, she has possessed
herself of her liberty, but yet she has retained that
gem beyond all price—her winsome womanhood,

the greatest and most powerful weapon for the subduing of man.

It is curious that the Burmese who are certainly in some ways so apparently civilised, should in others be almost barbaric in some of their customs. For example, on the birth of a child the Burmese mother is as nearly killed with what might be deemed kindness, but is in reality the most gross ignorance, as can possibly be conceived. Whatever the state of the weather, even if the thermometer stand at 110° or more, the miserable mother, directly the child is in the world, is placed as near to a huge fire as it is possible. Hot bricks, rugs, and blankets are piled upon her, and this she has to endure for seven days, besides drinking a noisome compound called Green Medicine. On the seventh day, the woman is given a kind of Turkish bath, which is in reality sitting over a vessel containing boiling water, into which has been put tamarind twigs, and a few other leaves of different kinds. After she has endured this for about an hour, still of course enveloped in the hot blankets, she is then given a cold bath, and is supposed after that to be cured, and able to resume her every-day duties. How she ever survives the treatment is indeed a marvel.

There is another treatment for a confinement which does not appear nearly as disagreeable, it is the following :—The patient has to drink a concoction made from three roots, called Isa-pa-lay, Orin-pya, Ka-doo-mi ma-kin. These three roots are pounded well together with an equal amount of each root, and this medicine is administered three times a day to the woman with cold water. They say that this medicine is very heating so

A BURMESE GIRL DRESSING HER HAIR.

that they are ordered to bathe in cold water three days after the confinement. It certainly sounds a more natural treatment, and one less calculated to kill quite so many patients.

There are certain whispers concerning the morality of these delightful little damsels, rumours which say that their standard on these points does not quite coincide with European ideas. Their affections are inclined to be a trifle catholic, and they have occasionally too generous a wish to

A DANCING GIRL POSTURING.

make the bungalows of certain poor exiles a little more homelike than is perhaps quite wise or quite necessary.

These little ladies do not discard the aid of paint
and powder, which is greatly to be deplored, as in
many cases they much disfigure their pretty little
faces, and do not in any way enhance their charms.
The powder they use is made from the bark and
roots of Murraya Paniculata, a kind of shrub of
the citron kind. They make it into a paste and
then smear it over the face. It is occasionally
used also by very smart young men !

Burmese women are not generally highly educated, and that seems the single instance of
their not possessing all the advantages of the
men. Learning is not considered necessary for a
woman. Perhaps her wits are considered sharp
enough without it, and any spare time that she
has they consider is better expended upon adorn-
ing herself. In Rangoon, however, among the
richer classes, the women are often very well
educated, and some are quite learned in Burmese
literature.

Now that I have arrived at the last page of my
chapter on these Burmese dames, I wonder if I
have succeeded in my efforts to do full justice to
their charms, and whether I have sufficiently
emphasised and dwelt upon their graces and
delightful personality. I would fain have you
love them as I do, and as you would, if you
could only walk with me down a street in
Rangoon or Mandalay, and behold them like so

many dainty coloured flowers, dotted here and there, all laughing, talking, joking, all telling you by their sweet joyous faces that life (anyhow in Burma) is worth living.

CHAPTER III.

AMONG the numerous picturesque objects which
Burma possesses, none are so graceful, or add
so much to the interest of the country and the
charm of the landscape, as the pagodas. These
fascinating, airy structures are to be seen in every
town and village. They peep up through every
grove of mango, they deck every hillside and river
bank. In design they are bell or conical shaped,
wide at the base and tapering gradually away until
they are surmounted by what is called a Htee or
Umbrella Spire. They are built usually of bricks,
and covered either with plaster or gold-leaf.

To erect one of these tapering, picturesque
edifices is to arrive at one of the greatest ambitions
of a Burman's life. It is supposed that the building of a pagoda will procure for him everything
that is delightful in the next world, and immense
cudos, reverence, and respect in this. In fact, it
would seem a charmingly facile manner of com-

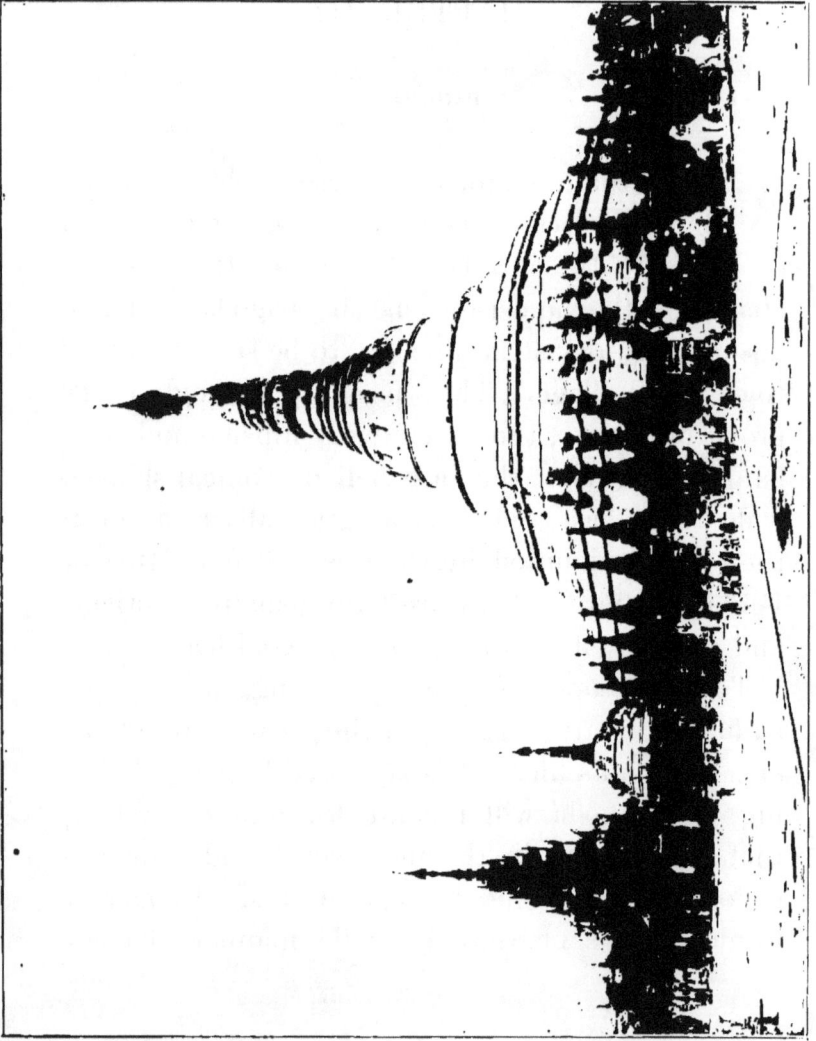

THE SHWAY DAGOHN.

passing the great difficulty of gaining joy in both worlds, and of serving God and Mammon.

The title of " Payah Tagah " (builder of a pagoda) is always added to the name of the virtuous individual who spends his money in this admirable way !

The word " pagoda " would signify " relic shrine," but the amount of these treasures would now indeed have to be as the sands of the sea if they are to equal the thousands of pagodas ! Pagodas in Burma are built in a solid mass except for what is called the Tapanah-teik, or relic-chamber, which is a square room built at the base of the shrine, and is the portion of the building that is usually completed first.

The most famous of these structures are the " Shway Dagohn " at Rangoon, the " Shway-San-Daw " at Prome, the " Shway-Hmaw-Daw " at Pegu—all these, it is steadfastly affirmed, contain holy hairs of Buddha !

The " Shway Dagohn " at Rangoon, or Golden Pagoda, is one of the most ancient and venerated shrines which exists, and it certainly should hold a high place among the beautiful and artistic monuments of the world, for it is exquisite in design and form. Its proportions and height are simply magnificent ; wide at the base, it shoots up 370 feet, tapering gradually away until crowned by its airy golden Htee, or umbrella-shaped roof.

This delicate little structure is studded profusely
with precious stones and hung round with scores
of tiny gold and jewelled bells, which, when
swung lightly by the soft breeze, give out the
tenderest and most mystic of melodies. The
Htee was the gift of King Mindohn-Min, and

VIEW OF THE GOLDEN PAGODA FROM DALHOUSIE PARK.

it is said to have cost the enormous sum of fifty
thousand pounds.

The great pagoda is believed by the faithful to
have been erected in 588 B.C.; but for many
centuries previous to that date the spot where the
pagoda now stands was held sacred, as the relics
of three preceding Buddhas were discovered there
when the two Talaing brothers (the founders of

the Great Pagoda) brought the eight holy hairs
of Buddha to the Thehngoothara Hill, the spot
where the pagoda now stands. Shway Yoe (Mr.
Scott) says that it also possesses in the Tapanah-
teik, or relic chamber, of the pagoda the drinking
cup of Kaukkathan, the "thengan," or robe, of
Gawnagohng, and the "toungway," or staff, of
Kathapah. It is therefore so holy that pilgrims
visit this shrine from far countries, such as Siam,
and even the Corea. The height of the pagoda
was originally only twenty-seven feet, but it has
attained its present proportions by being constantly
encased in bricks. It is a marvellously striking
structure, raising up its delicate, glittering head
from among a wondrous company of profusely
carved shrines and small temples, whose colour
and cunning workmanship make fit attendants to
this stupendous monument.

It is always a delight to one's eyes to gaze upon
its glittering spire, always a fairy study of artistic
enchantment; but perhaps if it has a moment
when it seems clothed with peculiar and almost
ethereal, mystic attraction, it is in the early
morning light, when the air has been bathed by
dewdrops and is of crystal clearness, and when that
scorching Eastern sun has only just begun to send
forth his burning rays. I would say go and gaze
on the pagoda at the awakening hour, standing
there on the last spur of the Pegu Hills, and

framed by a luxuriant tropical bower of foliage.
The light scintillates and glistens like a myriad of
diamonds upon its golden surface, and the dreamy
beauty of its glorious personality seems to strike
one dumb with deep, unspoken reverence and
admiration.

Nestling on one side of it are a number of

MONASTERIES AND REST-HOUSES ROUND THE GOLDEN PAGODA.

Pohn-gyee Kyoung (monasteries) and rest-houses
for pilgrims. All these are quaint, carved, and
gilded edifices from which you see endless yellow-
robed monks issuing. The monasteries situated
at the foot of the great pagoda seem peculiarly
harmonious, as if they would seek protection and

shelter beneath the wing of their great mother church.

The pagoda itself is approached on four sides by long flights of steps, but the southern is the principal entrance and that most frequented. At the base of this stand two gigantic lions made of brick and plastered over, and also decorated with coloured paint; their office is to guard the sacred place from nats (evil spirits) and demons, the fear of which seems ever to haunt the Burman's mind and be a perpetual and endless torment to him. From this entrance the steps of the pagoda rise up and are enclosed by a series of beautifully carved teak roofs, supported by wood and masonry pillars. There are several quaint frescoes of Buddha and saints depicted upon the ceiling of these roofs, but the steps which they cover are very rugged and irregular. It is, indeed, a pilgrimage to ascend them, although the foreigner is allowed to retain his shoes. The faithful, of course, leave theirs at the foot of the steps.

The entrance to the pagoda inspires one with a maze of conflicting emotions as one stands before it; joy, sorrow, pity, wonder, admiration follow so quickly upon each other that they mingle into an indescribable sense of bewilderment. The first sight of the entrance is gorgeous, full of Eastern colour and charm; and then sorrow and horror fill one's heart, as one's eyes fall suddenly upon the rows of lepers who line the way to the holy place. Each is a terrible, gruesome sight, a mass of ghastly corruption and disease, and each holds out with maimed, distorted hands a little tin vessel for your alms.

Why should Providence allow so awful an

SOUTHERN ENTRANCE TO THE GOLDEN PAGODA.

infliction as leprosy to fall upon His creatures? Could any crime, however heinous, be foul enough for such a punishment? These are the thoughts which flit through your brain; and then, as you pass on, wonder takes their place at the quaint beauty of the edifice, and lastly intense and wild admiration takes entire possession of you, and all

is forgotten in the glorious nearness of the great
Golden Pagoda.

On either side of the rugged steps there are
rows of most picturesque little stalls, at which are
sold endless offerings to be made to Buddha—
flowers of every shade and hue, fruit, glowing
bunches of yellow plantains and pepia, candles,
wondrous little paper devices and flags, and, lastly,
the gold leaf, which the faithful delight to place
upon the beloved pagoda. It is looked upon as a
great act of merit to expend money in thus decorating the much loved and venerated shrine.

There is a curious and melancholy history con-
nected with the people who hold these little stalls.
They are called "pagoda slaves," and they were
and are yet looked upon as outcasts; no respectable Burman would dream of holding any inter-
course with them, as it would be impossible for
him to do so without contamination. The pagoda
slaves are the descendants of prisoners taken in
war, but no king has had the power of liberating
them, and should a Burman marry one, even
unknowingly, he and any children he might have
by a previous marriage would become also pagoda
slaves. It is hoped that by degrees this curse
will be removed under our rule, but as things move
slowly in Burma, it will take time.

The history concerning these poor people is a
very singular one. It is as follows:—In the life-

time of Buddha there was a mighty king called Peam-na-tha-ryah, who reigned over a large city called Ya-ya-gne. One day it chanced that the king passed by the koung (monastery) and beheld the priest cleaning out the koung, and he stopped and asked if he would accept some men to do this menial office instead of himself as an offering. The priest replied that he could not accept the men without the consent of Buddha. Buddha answered that such an offering of men to serve the koung might be accepted. The king therefore offered fifty men to do service at the monastery.

After this offering it is said that the village flourished exceedingly, and it was ever after named Kapilawook (Kapi signifies offerings). This was the true origin of the pagoda slaves. No curse then rested upon them; theirs was a voluntary service, and they were exempt from the paying of taxes, and their one duty was to serve the monastery. But by degrees the idea of pagoda slaves changed, abuses crept in, and the pure, fair notion of the voluntary-service giver was forgotten, and kings took to offering the prisoners taken in war to the pagodas and koungs, and putting a terrible curse upon them—a curse so dreadful that no one had the power of releasing them from this merciless and barbarous slavery, which lasted through all their lives and descended to generations yet unborn. This punishment was

the most degrading and the most dreadful that
could be inflicted, and this slavery lasted for eight
hundred years, from the reign of King Manya-
tayaw to the annexation of Burma, and even now
continues in a lesser degree. The first king who
made his prisoners of war pagoda slaves was
Du-la-ka-ma, King of Ceylon. He conquered the
city of Chakim and brought the rebels to his
country, where, after cursing them, he offered
them to the Ta-de-daw pagoda as slaves. Naw-
ral-ta-ya, the famous King of Paghn (the Holy
City of Burma), who reigned about the time of
King Canute, conquered the King of Tha-tone,
from which country he brought the prisoners back
to Paghn; he then cursed them, and offered them
as slaves to the Thw-ye-gon Pagoda in his own
city.

Kyan-yil-tha, also King of Paghn a little later,
about the time of William the Conqueror, after he
became king, revenged himself upon his wife's
relations by cursing them and offering them as
pagoda slaves; this he did because they had called
him a pagoda slave in the days when he was
poor!

Later, again, in the reign of Charles I., Tha-lon-
Min-tayah, the King of Ava, first conquered the
Shans, and brought them as prisoners, whom he
cursed and offered to the Koung-mhoo-daw Pagoda
in Lagaing as pagoda slaves. This is the true

history and origin of the pagoda slaves, and a very strange and sad one it is. Sad that a custom which had begun with so much purity of thought and desire should sink to such terrible depths of horror and revenge, and though one trusts that by degrees this is passing away, it has not entirely done so at present, and probably it will take many years before the old curse can be forgotten.

Occasionally, I am told, a pagoda slave has with utmost difficulty concealed his birth, and gone into business in some large town; but he lives in constant dread of detection, and of being cast out from among respectable people. The majority of these pagoda slaves did not appear to make any effort to raise themselves, but accepted their fate, and still remained round the pagodas selling offerings to the devout. No pagoda slave was permitted to enter a monastery, nor would a Pohngyee (monk) even accept alms from one. No bait, be it money or anything that this world could give, could bring these poor people into communion with their fellows. A Burmese girl would not think of marrying one, not even if he possessed the riches of Golconda. Their position was a most strange and unique one, and not the least terrible part of it was the infectiousness of their curse, which descended upon those with whom they might wish (and who in their turn might have been willing), to hold converse with them.

Who can tell what tragic love-stories have per-chance been enacted between these poor outcasts and their more fortunate brothers; what heart-breakings and heart-burnings, and all unrecorded, borne in patience and perhaps in silence.

As you mount slowly up the steep uneven steps of the pagoda, turn for a moment and glance back

VIEW OF THE GOLDEN PAGODA FROM CANTONMENT GARDEN.

at the scene. It is a pagoda feast, and the place is crowded with the faithful from all parts, who have come from far and near to present offerings and perform their religious observances. It is an entrancing picture, a marvel of colour and pic-turesqueness—see, the stalls are laid out with their brightest wares, and the crowd is becoming

greater every moment. Look at that group of
laughing girls, they have donned their most
brilliant tamehns, and dainty shawls, and the
flowers in their hair are arranged with infinite
coquettishness ; behind them are coming a
dazzling company of young men in pasohs of
every indescribable shade ; perchance they are
the lovers of the girls whom they are following so
eagerly, and they are bearing fruit and flowers to
present to Buddha. Beyond them again are
some yellow-robed Pohn-gyees ; they are supposed
to shade their eyes from looking upon women with
their large lotus-shaped fans, but to-day they are
gazing about them more than is permitted, and
are casting covert glances of admiration on some
of those dainty little maidens. Behind them
again are a white-robed company, they are nuns,
and their shroud-like garments flow around them
in long graceful folds. Their hair is cut short,
and they have not so joyous an expression upon
their faces as the rest of the community, and they
toil up the steep steps a trifle wearily. Behind
them again are a little toddling group of children,
with their little hands full of bright glowing
flowers and fruit.

Shall we follow in the crowd and see where the
steps lead ? It is a wondrous study, the effects of
light and shade ; look at that sunbeam glinting in
through the roof and laying golden fingers on the

Pohn-gyees' yellow robes, and turning the soft-
hued fluttering silks into brilliant luminous spots
of light.

At last we have arrived at the summit! Let us
pause and take breath morally and physically before
walking round the great open-paved space in the
centre of which rises the great and glorious

SHRINES SURROUNDING THE GOLDEN PAGODA.

pagoda. There it stands towering up and up, as
though it would fain touch the blue heaven; it is
surrounded by a galaxy of smaller pagodas, which
seem to be clustering lovingly near their great
high priest; around these again are large carved
kneeling elephants, and deep urn-shaped vessels,
which are placed there to receive the offerings of

food brought to Buddha. The crows and the
pariah dogs which haunt the place will soon
demolish these devout offerings, and grow fat
upon them as their appearance testifies; but this,
curiously, does not seem in the least to annoy the
giver. He has no objection to seeing a fat crow
or a mangy dog gorging itself upon his offering,
as the feeding of any animal is an act of merit,
which is, the one thing of importance to a Burman.
The more acts of merit that he can accomplish in
this life, the more rapid his incarnations will be in
the next.

There are draped about the small golden pagodas
and round the base of the large one endless quaint
pieces of woven silk; these are offerings from
women, and must be completed in one night
without a break.

On the outer circle of this large paved space are
a multitude of shrines, enclosing hundreds of
images of Buddha. You behold Buddha standing,
you behold him sitting, you behold him reclining;
you see him large, you see him small, you see him
medium size; you see him in brass, in wood, in
stone, and in marble. Many of these statues are
simply replicas of each other, but some differ
slightly, though the cast of features is always the
same, a placid, amiable, benign countenance, with
very long lobes to the ears, which in Burma are
supposed to indicate the great truthfulness of the

person who possesses them. Most of the images
have suspended over them the royal white umbrella,

DOORWAY AT THE SUMMIT OF STEPS LEADING TO THE
GOLDEN PAGODA.

which was one of the emblems of Burma, and only
used in Thebaw's time to cover Buddha, the king,
and the lord white elephant.

Many of the shrines which enclose these images are exquisitely carved in teak wood and gilded. In design they are most elaborate, composed of grotesque figures of animals, nats, and demons; the profuse and lavish ornamentation of the work is absolutely marvellous.

One Chinese shrine, lately erected, struck me as particularly quaint. It was carved and painted with extraordinary minuteness, and with a multiplicity of people, flowers, birds, animals, &c., which was quite bewildering. The interior of this wonderful structure was decorated with weird pictures depicted upon rice-paper, and the whole shrine was supported upon beautifully ornamented bronze pillars. The pillars, though utterly incongruous with the florid carving and rich Eastern colours, did not harmonise so ill as might have been imagined. These shrines are erected by devout Buddhists as an act of merit.

There is a very curious company of bells of all sizes hung on short beams. Bells in Burma are not used to call to prayer, but rather to call attention to the fact, that the prayer has been said. After performing his religious observances the Burman strikes the bell to let Buddha and the nats know that he has performed his service.

The most interesting bell there is on the eastern side, enclosed in a wooden shed. It weighs 94,682 lbs. Its history is quite unique; it was presented

to the pagoda by King Tharrawaddy in 1840.
After the second Burmese war, the English conceived the barbarous and shameful idea of removing
it to Calcutta as a trophy; but mercifully this
vandalism was averted by the bell, in its transit,
falling into the river at Rangoon. Numerous
were the attempts made by English engineers to

THE GREAT BELL AT THE GOLDEN PAGODA.

raise the bell, but all to no purpose. There it
remained safely reposing at the bottom of the
river. After some years had elapsed, the Burmans
tendered a request that they might have the sacred
bell restored to them on the condition that they
they could recover it. Their petition was granted
with sneering amusement, the bare idea of a

6

Burman succeeding where an Englishman had failed was too ridiculous to contemplate! But for once we must allow ourselves beaten. Victory attended the Burmans' efforts, and after many exertions, their labours were crowned with success, and the bell was raised and borne back triumphantly to the pagoda, where, we will trust, it will ever remain.

The scene all round the great Golden Shrine is one of peculiar interest; one could spend hours wandering round and round gazing on the wonders of carving, and on the ceaseless crowd which comes and goes, like an ever-changing panorama. Here you see a charming company of Burmans before a shrine, looking up towards the image while they recite their prayers, while close beside them is a lovely little family group—a woman with a few roses which she has brought as her gift to Buddha, and beside her is her husband with a bunch of warm yellow bananas, and close to him the tiny child holding out a quaint little paper flag. There is something singularly touching about their worship; it is all performed with the utmost reverence and simplicity, and their intense earnestness and child-like faith impresses you with the sincerity of their wish to present Buddha of their best.

In another corner of the large paved space your gaze lights upon a very typical group of Burmans.

You would say by their expressions that something
of very great importance was taking place, and so
it is in their eyes. They have all gathered round
a fortune-teller, who has been drawing the horo-
scope of one of the party, and the friends are
waiting with evident anxiety to hear the result,
and then to offer their congratulations or con-
dolences as the case may require.

The Burmese are the most superstitious of
people. The choice of a lucky day or a lucky hour,
the consulting of soothsayers, the wearing of
charms, all play a most important part in their
lives, and possess a marvellously strong hold upon
their imaginative natures. It is curious that this
fortune-telling and seeking to pierce the veil of
the future should even show itself boldly in the
holiest place, and follow in the wake of their
religious observances, as it is quite a matter of
hourly occurrence for a Burman, after repeating
his prayers, to then betake himself to a fortune-
teller and inquire of him a lucky day or hour in
which he may marry, commence to build a house,
or cut his paddy. So strong is their belief in these
wise men that nothing would persuade them to
enter upon any important enterprise without first
ascertaining the exact day and hour upon which it
would be lucky to begin. All round the pagoda
you see these soothsayers, seated with their books
and their charts ready to be consulted.

There is a curious legend told in regard to the founding of the great Golden Pagoda.

The founders of this celebrated shrine are supposed to have been the two Talaing brothers of the names of Taposa and Palecka. They received from Buddha eight sacred hairs from his beard, and he then instructed them to deposit these holy relics on the Thchngoottara Hill, beside the relics of the three preceding Buddhas, which were already there.

The two happy brothers started off joyfully to search for this holy spot, but for some time their quest was utterly in vain, and though they travelled many weary miles they yet could nowhere discover where the spot lay. At length, when they were becoming utterly downcast, and giving up all hope of success, the king of the Tha-gyhs took pity upon them and descended from heaven in the guise of a nat (spirit) and appeared to the disheartened brothers, who rejoiced exceedingly at the sight of him. He told them that the holy spot for which they were searching lay near to their native land, and that the only person who could direct them to it was a nat of great age, called Soolay. To him the brothers forthwith betook themselves, but he was of so great an age that his eyelashes had grown to such an extraordinary length that they lay upon the ground, and he was unable to lift his lids and look upon the light of day. When the

THE SULAY PAGODA.

brothers told him their errand, and begged for help
in discovering the sacred hill, he grew suspicious
and pleaded blindness. But the brothers were not
easily to be baffled; they saw that before his aid
could be invoked the lids of his eyes would have to
be supported, and as he was a nat of giant stature
this could only be effected by the hewing down of
young trees, which they shaped into props to bear
the heavy lids. When this had been achieved,
the light of day fell upon the eyes of the aged
nat, and he directed them to the Thehngoottara
Hill, where the sacred spot was found.

It is a quaint picturesque legend, full of local
colour and imagination, as are most of the things
which have to do with the Burmese.

There are many pagodas at Rangoon, the Sulay,
close to the quay, being one of the most picturesque, but they are all small, and sink into insig-
nificance beside the great Shway Dagohn.

Every pagoda of any note has its feast day.
And these pagoda feasts are the red-letter days and
great holidays of the Burmans. As these naturally
occur very frequently, seeing that the number of
pagodas is nearly as numerous in Burma as the
sands of the sea, holidays in that blessed country
seem to form the largest portion of the year. The
greatest pagoda feast, and the one of by far the
most consequence is, of course, that held at the
great Golden Pagoda at Rangoon; but it has now

become too civilised, and is not nearly so picturesque as those held in the more remote country
places. There are two or three pagodas within
ten or twelve miles of Rangoon where the feasts
are most picturesque. These are, in fact, a real
al fresco picnic, which lasts for a day or two ; and
here joy, laughter, and amusement hold carnival.
Amusement always manages to creep in, and in
fact generally protrudes itself, and holds a very
prominent position wherever a Burman is con-
cerned. Therefore at a pagoda feast religion and
entertainment go hand in hand. It is there that
the old can meet and gossip, that the middle-aged
can discuss the crops and the market price of
paddy, and it is there that the young can make
love. After the religious ceremony has been performed and they have solemnly visited the pagoda,
they can then sit in the shade, or saunter through
the cool dark jungle, whispering soft vows of con-
stancy, and many a young man's heart has been lost
and many a maiden's heart won at a pagoda feast.
In the evening under the clear moonlight the Pwè
takes place, and then merriment, jocosity, and
frivolity takes entire possession of the company.
The devout travel to these pagoda feasts in bullock
carts, and charmingly picturesque they look. A
whole family packed comfortably away in these
quaint, roomy conveyances, which have a most
picturesque awning over them, composed of bent

bamboo, upon which is thrown a brilliant coloured
piece of tapestry or rug. These carts are much
prettier and more decorated in Upper Burma,
though they are very heavy, as sometimes the
wheels are constructed of solid pieces of wood, and
occasionally these wheels are cut square, the
corners being allowed to work off. These solid
wheels also squeak in a most abominable and
excruciating manner, which the owners do not
object to, as they are thus warned of the near
approach of another cart; and it is even said that
they know their friends by the particular squeak
of his wheels! Another curious thing about the
pagodas, and one which strikes a stranger as
very peculiar, is the enormous quantity of ruined
shrines that are to be seen. The reason for this
is, that repairing a pagoda (except it be one of the
most venerated shrines) brings no merit to the
restorer, but all merit goes to the original founder,
hence the explanation of the brilliant new pagoda
next to most dilapidated and miserable structures.
When a pagoda has been erected, there is, generally,
a kind of dedication service. But for this there are
no actual rules laid down in the sacred books, so that
it is left to the imagination and will of the Pohn-
gyee who performs the service. There is always a
good deal of almsgiving and pouring out of water
drop by drop, which is to show that the Koothat
or merit falls upon all present. Besides all the

religious part, there is, of course, the usual amusement, which no Burman festival could do without.
The architecture of the pagodas in Lower Burma
is, as a rule, much simpler, and does not possess
nearly as much ornamentation as in Upper Burma,
where there are some evidences of really great
architectural efforts.

CHAPTER IV.

BEFORE leaving Rangoon and asking you to accompany me further up-country, there are a few miscellaneous subjects upon which I should like to say a few words.

First, the elephants, whose work in the great teak yards of Rangoon is a most curious and striking feature.

These wonderful animals performing their daily task of stacking timber is really a marvellous sight, quite, I maintain, in its way, one of the most interesting to be witnessed anywhere. We spent a most delightful hour in Mr. MacGregor's timber yard at Rangoon, watching these truly extraordinary creatures, whose instinct—or may I call it mind?—is something astounding. They lift the huge teak logs by the aid of their tusks and trunks, and pile them up one upon another, with the most amazing precision, in such a manner that the ends of each plank are quite on a line with one another.

91

When a log is of too great a weight for one elephant to manipulate, another comes and tenders his aid, and together they hoist the huge beam into its place. They drag up the very large planks from the river by the aid of a chain, and this they undo in the cleverest manner imaginable.

ELEPHANTS AT WORK STACKING TIMBER.

The chain is fastened round the wood by means of a hook, and this the elephants shake until it becomes detached. It occasionally happens that the hook gets jammed and is difficult to undo. When this is the case I have been told that the elephant has actually been known to carefully

bend it out with the help of his feet and trunk in
the most cunning way, until it can be detached.
It is affirmed that the elephants become so cute
that they are able to distinguish the good logs
from the bad ones! and there is a saying at
Maulmein that the elephants there shut one eye

ELEPHANT PUSHING A LOG INTO POSITION.

and look along the beams to assure themselves
that they are quite horizontal! They certainly
have a curiously precise manner of pushing the
logs into their exact angle, as if anything that·was
not quite parallel hurt their sense of neatness.
Each elephant has a man upon his head but these

men do practically nothing, for a really well
trained elephant knows his work perfectly, and
elephants which are trained are worth about five
thousand rupees.

The next thing, which at Rangoon is a great
feature, and adds much to the pleasure, and I
think I may say, to the health of the inhabitants,

DALHOUSIE PARK.

is the Dalhousie Park. It is a large and beautifully
designed public garden. A great portion of this
was planned and carried out by Major Temple, son
of the late Governor of Bombay, and now himself
Governor of the Andaman Islands. It does him
enormous credit, for the landscape gardening and
arrangement is admirably conceived. For its size

it is quite one of the most picturesque and charming drives to be seen anywhere. The gardens
encircle a large lake, whose lines are broken by
fascinating little islands, and the shores are
cunningly devised and arranged in delicately cut
little bays, and lovely miniature creeks.

The road winds in and out along this cool,

DRIVE BY THE SIDE OF THE LAKE IN DALHOUSIE PARK.

rippling expanse of water, over which a cool breeze
nearly always blows. On this lake float many
charming pleasure boats, some rowed by gay
laughing groups, and others skim along with
their glittering sails set, looking like large white
birds.

On the other side of this delightful drive lies an

undulating park-like pleasaunce of exquisite green sward, which wanders away until lost in a dreamy tropical grove of palms, from which the stupendous pagoda rears its stately head.

It is here that the band discourses sweet music, while the *beau monde* of Rangoon disports itself either by floating lazily on the silvery waters of the lake, or by driving round its shores behind the fascinating little Burman ponies, whose nimble little feet carry them swiftly through the delicious cool evening breeze.

These ponies are another very distinct feature of Burma; they are generally about eleven to thirteen hands high, and are very sturdy little creatures, and also fairly fast. As they are considered extremely good for polo ponies, and are also used for racing purposes, they look very quaint drawing the enormous gharrys (cabs), but they move these rather ponderous vehicles without apparently the least effort. They are occasionally rather wilful little people. A pair of them belonging to our host, Mr. Smeaton, were most entertaining. I am convinced that they used to make little plots together for turning down some particular road, as they put their funny little heads quite close and whispered to each other, and then, if you were not on the look out, swish you would go round some corner that you had no intention of penetrating into. They were most grotesque in their behaviour on their

return home from a drive. They were in the
habit of having a banana bestowed upon them,
and the eager way in which they turned round to
look for the dainty, and the absolutely reproachful
expression they assumed, if by any chance the
fruit was not forthcoming, was really most comical
and human.

There is another animal in Burma which, in its
own way, has quite as distinct a right to be
mentioned as the ponies, as it is, I am informed, an
entirely Burman product, and that is a tucktoo.

In appearance it resembles a large lizard, and
it is looked upon as extremely lucky if a tucktoo
thinks you worthy of domiciling himself beneath
your roof. He also makes himself useful, as he
devours the flies and mosquitoes, and small vermin
of that kind, which is much to be commended.
He possesses the most weird, I might almost say
blood-curdling, cry, that I have ever heard. I had
been told a great deal about the tucktoo, but the
days passed away and I never succeeded in hearing
him discourse, and it was not until the very last
night of my stay in Burma that I actually did so.
I was dressing for dinner when Mrs. Smeaton's
Aya rushed into my room and begged that the
Memsaib would come at once into the next room,
as the tucktoo was talking. I hurried off, but, alas!
by the time I arrived, the tucktoo had ceased his
conversation, and I returned quite disheartened and

hopeless of ever hearing him. That night, however,
I was awakened suddenly by the strangest and
most gruesome cries I have ever heard. I listened
for a moment, and then suddenly I realised that
it was the tucktoo which was talking. At last
I had really heard him. He seemed to exclaim,
in the most vociferous, cracked voice, the word
"Tucktoo, tucktoo, tucktoo," repeated several
times over, beginning high up the scale and running gradually down until it died away in a
curious low melancholy groan, which made one
feel shivery, and conjured up weird dreams of
Dante's Inferno, it seemed so like the cry of a
lost, wandering soul.

There is a very curious festival in Burma, called
the Water Festival. This festival takes place at
the Buddhist new year, about the beginning of
April, and it is the custom for the inhabitants to
perambulate the streets bearing small bowls of
water and little squirts, which latter they dis-
charge and level at the passers-by. It is also the
custom to go to people's houses and souse them
with water, of course in quite a friendly sort of
way. In fact it is considered a great compliment,
and those who do not receive this wetting are
quite hurt! The little Burmese girls enjoy these
Water Festivals enormously, and take the keenest
delight in this amusement, eagerly surrounding
any unfortunate man or woman whom they may

encounter, and not allowing them to depart on their way without a good shower bath. The exact origin of this quaint, and not altogether pleasant, custom, does not seem to be known, but two or three very fantastic legends are told with regard to it. One of these is the following :—" That the weight

THE LAKE, DALHOUSIE PARK.

of the world has been borne by a mortal for the space of a year as a punishment for sin, and that the water is used as a purification after the burden has been removed."

Another legend which is more fanciful, and more attractive, states that the world has been guarded

for a year by an angel, and that at the end of that
period the angel washes out all the sins of the past
year before delivering the world over to the protection of his successor.

Lieut.-General Fytche relates another legend
which tells of a king's head being washed by seven
nats who are the guardians of time, and these nats
are believed to pass on the king's head from one to
another as the old year dies and the new year
begins.

They are all singularly quaint, and point to the
element of romance and imagination which is certainly so strongly marked in the Burman character.

The whole festival much resembles a carnival
with the difference that water is used instead of
flowers and confetti, and it is certainly a question
whether it is not better to be soused with water
than be nearly blinded with hard, uncompromising
confetti! I personally incline to the former,
especially in a climate like Burma, where the sun
with kindly thoughtfulness soon rectifies any moist
feeling that you may have.

The New Year's feast is a great and important
fête, and is observed all over Burma. It takes
place generally during the first days of April, but
it is rather a movable festival as the date of the
New Year was formerly fixed by the astrologers and
had to be arrived at by many minute calculations
to do with the heavenly bodies. It is now, I

believe, since our annexation, settled by one of the Government officials.

The fanciful idea is, that on every New Year the King of the Tha-gyahs descends upon the earth as a herald of the birth of a new season, and there are all sorts of curious superstitions about him with regard to what he will bring with him. For instance, should he make his appearance with a sword, war and misery will be the prophecy of the coming year; if with a vessel of water, that the rains will fall at the right time and the crops will be good. They also conceive the strange notion that he comes riding upon a beast, and it is of great significance what kind of an animal he rides upon. Should he come upon a " nagah " a very wet season is foretold, or should he come upon a " galohu," terrible and violent storms will be the fate of the country, but if he should make his entry in homely fashion upon his feet and bearing a lantern, the heat will be overpowering. This fantastic idea goes on to imagine that he will spend a few days upon earth, the term of his visit being determined by the wise men. At length when all is at last arranged, and it must, one would imagine, take a good deal of thinking out, the astrologers give the signal and the king makes his appearance, all the people are on the watch for this great event armed with jars of water. Whether many of them imagine that they really see the great sight or are bitterly disappointed at beholding nothing I do not know. They pour out their water, repeat a prayer and seem quite satisfied and believe that the great and awful personage has come down to earth. The Dewah king has the very uncomfortable habit of arriving just at midnight, which seems a very thoughtless proceeding on his part, as he keeps so many good people out of their beds! A few retire to rest after the descent is made, but others remain up the whole night.

At the first moment that the sun makes his appearance, when the first wistful light of morn begins to show itself, the faithful rise and, bearing vessels containing pure clean water, they betake themselves to the monasteries and present to the monks. This presentation means an asking for pardon for past sins and is also given as an offering to the brethren. After this ceremony has been duly performed, they proceed to the pagoda and there takes place the washing of the images. This is also done more as an act of respect than that they consider that in any moral way the images require cleansing. After this the real fun of the day takes place, and the Water Festival begins in good earnest.

They have another curious custom with regard to the rains. When the time arrives that the welcomed moisture should fall, and it does not

appear, they weave a long garland, and this they
drag along the road with the vain and illusive
hope that it may tempt the recalcitrant water to
descend.   When this device fails in bringing
about the desired effect, they take the wreath up
to the pagoda, and there the priest measures it;
if it should reach the whole way round the pagoda,
they are quite satisfied, as it is then supposed that
the rain must of necessity come.   As this ceremony is only performed at the time when the
monsoon is about to break, they are happily not
often disappointed.

Another very picturesque object at Rangoon are
the European bungalows.   They struck me as far
more picturesque and unique than those in India,
and being mounted upon piles to keep them dry
during the great rainfall, gives them a very distinct character.   They are constructed entirely of
wood, and are built rather upon the pattern of a
Swiss châlet, with the delightful overhanging
roofs, deep eaves and large square porchlike
verandahs.   At Rangoon they are nearly always
surrounded with the most lovely tropical growth
of trees, and many have exquisite gardens.   The
vegetation at Rangoon is very striking, the luxuriance and growth of the trees and shrubs, and the
intense green fills one with amazement, especially
after the arid plains of· India.   The pineapple
fields at Rangoon are another very curious sight,

they extend over some acres, and present a very quaint appearance.

The climate of Rangoon in the winter is very pleasant, and though in the middle of the day it is very hot, the mornings and evenings are deliciously cool. In the rains it is a most trying place. Day after day of rain which never ceases, or even modifies, but falls in a solid mass of water, and the damp of your clothes, books, furniture, &c., is something beyond expression. It is almost impossible to keep the mould from getting upon every article even though you have a little stove inside your wardrobes, and the things are taken out every day, in fact it is quite an occupation airing your clothes. The moisture and mildew appear to find their way into everything, and lay horrible clammy hands upon all your choicest treasures. Earthquakes are rather objectionable visitors to Burma, and were, during the last year or so, very annoying in their frequency. We were fortunate enough (as it is always as well to have an experience) to feel a slight one while at Rangoon, but it was only a mild shiver, which simply had the effect of opening all the doors.

The Burman's idea of an earthquake is a very quaint one. They believe that the world has been borne upon the shoulders of four animals, who occasionally become weary of their burden and desire to shift the weight into a more comfortable

A EUROPEAN BUNGALOW.

position, hence it is when this change is being effected that the disagreeable result ensues!

With regard to the healthiness of Burma, I should like to say a few words. The people residing in Burma tell you how fortunate they are to be living there and not in India, as Burma is so much more healthy. While the people in India tell you exactly the reverse, and dilate upon what a pestilential place Burma is, and how unfortunate any one is to be stationed there, until you feel inclined to cry, " What is truth ? " Probably both ideas are exaggerated, and the great differences between the healthiness or unhealthiness of the two countries is not so great as they imagine. In the rains, or rather, after the rains, when the ground is saturated with moisture, Rangoon and the lower parts of Burma must be extremely trying, the miasma and feverish mists which exude from the ground must of necessity be extremely deleterious and hurtful to European constitutions, and the statistics show that the heaviest mortality takes place in July and August after the monsoon. The healthiest months are generally considered to be February, March, and April; April is especially healthy. Fever is, of course, the illness that is most prevalent in Burma, and the mortality from that is higher than from any other disease. A most excellent system is now being introduced of selling quinine at the post-offices in all the native

villages and through local vendors, and we trust
that this will by degrees filter through and reach
the quite far out-lying provinces and districts,
which will be an immense blessing in staying the
ravages of this disease. Cholera appears much as it
does in India, but seems to be most prevalent along
the sea coast and in the states of Lower Burma,

CARTS BEING LOADED WITH PINEAPPLES.

and to leave the higher districts and river banks
comparatively much more free. The history of
cholera appears to bear a great resemblance all
over the world, and among its most striking
features are its prevalence amongst insanitary
surroundings and its wide spread, and notwithstanding this, its curious limitation to a comparatively small number of villages, especially in the

numerous centres of population which are so largely
dependent upon shallow wells for their water
supply. Smallpox is another ill from which
Burma is not exempt, and the vaccination which
is now being enforced is not as yet of universal
prevalence, nor has it succeeded in entirely
driving out the former practice of inoculation.

One of the great causes why so large a proportion
of fever and cholera and suchlike diseases arises
among the Burmese is from the thinness of their
clothing, and because they make a very small
addition to this in the winter and in the wet
season.

There have been most excellent sanitary laws
laid down by the Government for every village.

The following are a few of the regulations :—

" The headman shall not allow any house or
land in any village under his control to be, or to
be kept, in a filthy or insanitary condition, or to be
overgrown with weeds or rank vegetation.

" The headman shall not allow the corpse of a
human being, unless embalmed or unless enclosed
in an air-tight coffin, to be kept unburied or uncremated for more than forty-eight hours on any
house or land in any village under his control,
without the special sanction in each case of the
civil surgeon, sub-divisional officer, or township
officer. Provided that between the first day of
November and last day of February inclusive,

corpses may be kept unburied or uncremated for seventy-two hours.

"The headman shall not allow the corpse of a human being who has died of cholera, smallpox, or other infectious or contagious disease, to be kept for more than six hours unburied or uncremated on any house or land in any village under his control.

" The headman shall not allow the burning or burying of the corpse of a human being in, or the depositing of the same at, any place in any village under his control, except in a public burial ground, or a place set apart for that purpose by the township officer.

" The headman shall at once send a report to the nearest police station or outpost of the occurrence in any village under his control of cholera or smallpox, if two cases occur in close succession.

" When a corpse is interred it shall be buried at a depth of at least five feet not within thirty yards of any well, tank, or stream, or of any dwelling house; and the headman exercising control over the village where the interment takes place shall be bound to satisfy himself that this is done.

" The headman shall set apart in each village under his control one or more wells for drinking purposes, and shall cause to be constructed round each well either a parapet two feet high or a substantial hedge, and shall not allow bathing or washing of clothes within ten yards of any such well, and shall not allow the ground within ten yards of such wells to be defiled by filth, rubbish, or otherwise.

"If the water supply is from tanks, the headman shall reserve one tank for drinking purposes only, shall keep clean the banks thereof, and shall not allow bathing, washing of clothes, or watering of cattle in it.

"The headman shall cause the streets and lanes in each village under his control to be kept free from weeds, in good order, and in a sanitary condition.

"The headman shall mark out a place near, but outside, each village under his control, where rubbish may be deposited, and shall cause the rubbish to be burnt or worked into the land at ploughing time.

"The headman shall not allow a new house to be built in any village under his control within twenty feet of the front or back, or six feet of the side of any existing house."

These are all, no doubt, most excellent precepts to be followed, and they are highly to be commended, but whether the charming, easy-going Burman will ever trouble his head about them is very, very doubtful; and I should imagine, from what I know of him, that it will take many centuries to teach him any sanitary science; and certainly any government will be much to be congratulated who can bring the Burmese to practise real sanitation!

The ivory carving and the beaten silver work are both good at Rangoon. The carving in ivory, though not nearly as fine as the Japanese, is still decidedly quaint and original. The beaten silver work is one of the most important and beautiful things if done by really good workmen. We were fortunate enough to be told of a charming Burman, who lived in a very small shop and worked at the silver himself. He was a real artist, and his work had a delicacy and finish about it which is often sadly lacking in many of the Burmese silver bowls, which are frequently very rough and much wanting in clearness of outlines.

There are also very curious and grotesque articles called Kätägas, which are eminently a Burman product. These are pieces of black cloth or velvet, upon the surface of which are depicted the most quaint figures and scenes. These are produced and represented by pieces of brilliant coloured cloth or velvet, being cut out and stitched on to the cloth with an infinity of gold tinsel and a multiplicity of spangles. Some of these are very gorgeous and startling, and, though tawdry, if you examine them very closely, they are from a distance often extremely effective. The real use for them was, I believe, for a covering or pall for the bier.

At Mandalay I was taken into a native house where they were working these Kătăgas. They are done entirely by hand, the cloth being stretched tightly upon a frame so as to prevent any puckering of the material when the pieces are stitched upon it. They often show a great deal of ingenuity and imagination.

The wood carving is, perhaps, among the most prominent of Burman arts. It is marvellously quaint and partakes thoroughly of the native character, as it is most curious and imaginative. On the exterior of buildings it is extremely effective and charming, and has a great fascination. It is wonderfully profuse and lavish in its extraordinary minuteness and mass of figures and animals, but when you bring it within a building and examine it very closely, it oftentimes lacks finish and sharpness of moulding. It is all done in teak wood.

Among the most striking things in Burma are the Pwès (native plays). They are assuredly one of the things of the greatest importance, as they are the great national amusement of the country.

A Pwè takes place on every possible, and impossible, occasion in a Burman's life—when he is born, when he is baptised, when he marries, when a girl's ears are bored (for her first earrings) or a boy tattooed, when he erects a pagoda, and, lastly, when the final call comes, and he makes his exit

8

from this world. It is a Pwè which ushers the
Burman into life, and a Pwè which bows him out
of it again. These Pwès are always given in the
open air, and are free to any person who may desire
to witness them. A rough shed is generally erected,
in the centre of which they nearly always arrange
to have a tree. The exact reason for this I do not

A COUNTRY PWÈ

know. Whether it is simply as a background or
elementary scenery, or whether it has any mystic
significance, they were unable to tell me. The
favourite place for these representations seemed
to be the middle of the street (in front generally
of the giver's house), quite regardless of the traffic
which was impeded; that difficulty did not appear

to present itself to them, and fortunately the Burman "bobby" does not seem to enforce the ominous words of "Move on!"

Every Burman is more or less of an actor, and possesses undoubted dramatic power, and probably you would hardly discover one who had not at some time in his life taken part in these dramas. These Pwès are usually quite a variety entertainment, as there is singing, acting, dancing, or rather posturing, and a certain amount of jocosity, in which a clown takes part. The jokes are anything but refined, and are, to judge from some of the gestures, often extremely broad. The best professional troupes are at Rangoon and Mandalay; some are extremely good, and the whole *mise en scène* very effective, though the long fanciful stories, which generally tell of the many hundred previous existences of "Thin Gautama," or the fortunes of some fairy prince, are difficult for a European to follow or dissect. These plays, like the early drama, often take days to perform. The music, which is a great part of them, is extremely difficult for a European to grasp, as the tunes appear to have no tune, or else seem to go on always with the same monotonous refrain, which repeats itself over and over again.

The dancing, or posturing, is the most attractive part of a Pwè, and one of these dances, when really well performed by a pretty troup of girls in their brilliant coloured tamehns, is most effective. The Burmese are also very fond of marionette shows, which are nearly, if not quite, as popular as the Pwès. Anything, in fact, in the dramatic form seems to prove marvellously attractive to them.

GIRLS DANCING AT A PWÈ.

CHAPTER V.

MANDALAY.

THE distance between Rangoon and Mandalay measures some 386 miles, but, as the trains in Burma proceed at a slow, not to say dignified speed, the journey takes about twenty-two hours to accomplish.

The existing State Railway in Burma now extends from Rangoon to Mandalay, and up the Mu Valley *ria* Sagaing and Naha Kaung to Mohnyin, a distance in all of 627 miles,* and the further extension to Mogaung and Myitkina is well in hand. The branch from Maha Kaung to Katha on the Irrawaddy has also been opened for traffic.

The further extension of the Burma railways will have two main objectives. First, there is the much needed connection with the Indian system, either by way of Chittagong, Allyab, and Minbla, or starting from some higher point on the Assam

---

* This does not include the line from Rangoon to Prome, 161 miles.

Bengal Railway. Nothing definite has so far been settled with regard to this project. Secondly, the question of railway communication up to the Yunnan frontier has been under the consideration of the Government of India ever since the annexation of Upper Burma, and a step in this direction has recently been taken by the sanction given by the Secretary of State to the construction of a line from Mandalay *viâ* Thibaw to Kunlon Ferry on the Salween. The length of this line will probably be 270 miles, and it may cost about 225 lakhs of rupees.

Another direction in which railway extension in Burma has been advocated is from one of the Burmese ports towards the head of the Menam Valley. Such a railway would not, however, lie, for much of its length, in British territory, and no decision has yet been passed on this question.

The country lying immediately round Rangoon cannot be said to possess any very striking features of interest. Long tracts of rice-fields stretch for miles and miles, and these present a very desolate appearance, excepting just at the moment when the paddy is green; when they then possess a certain cool freshness. As you leave Lower Burma and proceed into Upper Burma, the country becomes far more attractive. Bamboos grow in the most splendid luxuriance; at some places weaving themselves into a dense, almost im-

penetrable jungle, which, though fascinating to
look upon, would hardly be agreeable to get
through.

On approaching Mandalay the country improves
still further, and becomes exceedingly charming.
The hills draw quite near, and are crowned with
hundreds of dainty little pagodas, and many small

BIRD'S-EYE VIEW OF MANDALAY AND THE SEVEN HUNDRED AND
SEVENTY-SEVEN PAGODAS.

native villages. Wherever you cast your eye the
spires of these lovely little shrines shoot up. Here
a solitary one stands out on the crest of a hill, or
a delicate company of them are gathered together
in the midst of a grove of palms and bananas.

Mandalay itself is a curiously unfinished place.
It rather resembles an overgrown village which

appears to have had the ambition to become a city, and yet which has not at present had the power to accomplish it. It is a finely conceived town, with broad streets and trees planted on either side, giving them the appearance of boulevards; but it is as it were only the figure of a town with some of the appurtenances of greatness and yet lacking the essential and vital parts. Mandalay is of mere mushroom growth, as it was only commenced in 1858. It was planned and laid out by King Mindohn Min, Thebaw's father. It was the last of many capitals which the kings of Burma had founded. Old Paghn, Tagoun, Mohtshobah, Amarapoora, and Ava having been among the many cities which had enjoyed the honour of being, for a time, the seat of government.

At the founding of any new capital in Burma there was a most ghastly ceremony performed. It was the custom to bury alive a certain number of people in the new walls of the city about to be erected, the idea for this horrible practice being that the spirits of these unfortunates became what are called Nat Thehn, and haunted the spot where their bodies lay, and thus proved a protection to the city, and scared any strangers who might come with evil intent. These miserable victims had to be selected from persons of a certain status, and it was also obligatory that they should have been born upon a certain day in the week. They were

usually chosen from young girls who had not their
ears bored, and boys who were guiltless of any
tattoo marks upon them.

When it was made known that victims were
required for this gruesome sacrifice, the streets
became absolutely denuded of inhabitants, excepting when they went about in strong bands,
which the officials did not venture to molest.
The idea of being buried alive naturally had not
a very inspiriting effect upon them, and did
not hold out great attractions! At those times
the Court would institute magnificent dramatic
entertainments in order to try and tempt the
people out of their hiding, but even that most
loved and cherished form of amusement failed to
entice them, and not a soul attended. The efficacy
of this gruesome practice was only supposed to
endure for a certain period, at the end of which
time it became absolutely necessary to repeat the
sacrifice.

Fifty persons, it is affirmed, were buried alive
at the founding of Mandalay. Four of these
miserable creatures were buried under each of the
twelve gates of the city; one at each of the four
corners, and the others being distributed in
different parts, and four being placed under the
throne itself. With the four who were buried at
the four corners were placed four jars of oil which
were securely fastened down, so that the weight of

the earth might not injure them. These jars were
supposed to indicate whether the sacrifice were
still efficacious, and they were examined at certain
intervals by the astrologers, if they were found full
and remained intact, all was supposed to be going
well, but if any of them should be found to be
empty, it was then believed necessary to procure
fresh victims. In 1880 two of these jars were said
to have been found without any oil in them, and at
that time a fearful scourge of smallpox appeared
in Mandalay, and many other misfortunes and bad
omens were said to have made their appearance.
So after much consultation with soothsayers and
astrologers it was determined to repeat the horrible
sacrifice; only this time it was to be repeated on
a much larger scale. The gruesome idea was
absolutely suggested of burying a hundred men,
a hundred women, a hundred boys, a hundred
girls, a hundred soldiers, and a hundred foreigners.
When this terrific announcement was spread
abroad it naturally produced a panic in the city,
and the inhabitants began to flee in all directions;
the river was crowded with boats, and the few
so-called tracks were filled with carts full of
fugitives striving to escape from so horrible a
doom, so that the city was in a fair way to be
utterly deserted. The ministers took fright at this;
and at the indignation of the English, which they
were told was great at the rumour of these

massacres, and they therefore countermanded
them, and strove to deny the whole thing. It
was rumoured, however, that many people had
been arrested, and that at the dead of night some
of them had been actually buried alive at each of
the posts of the twelve gates.

This was supposed to keep the spirits in a good
humour! and to be kept so secret that it would
not reach the ears of the much dreaded English.

The houses in Mandalay are nearly all native
bamboo dwellings, with the exception of the European bungalows, and a certain number of brick
houses; but the latter are decidedly in the minority
at present.

In King Thebaw's time brick buildings were not
permitted, as it was feared that in time of in-
surrection or war they might be turned into for-
tresses. The shape and style of a Burman's house
was arranged for him by law in Thebaw's time,
according to his position in society; gilding or any
ornamentation in lacquer was only permitted to a
few favoured officials, and an arch over the door
was forbidden to every one. It is curious to compare the rich elaborate architecture of the pagodas
and monasteries, with the very simple, almost
rude, bamboo dwellings in which the Burman
lives. Probably the very strict rules laid down
for the construction of these houses prevented any
original ideas from showing themselves; and later,

the conservative feeling, which is so strong a part
of the Burman, has prevented him striking out
any new lines, and thus changing the architecture
of his abode, which is to be deplored when you
see the skill that they evidently possess.

The native dwellings possess a certain pictu-

A BURMAN HOUSE.

resqueness; they are built of bamboo. The walls
are matting woven from the fibre of bamboo. The
exact pattern of this matting was also regulated by
law in Thebaw's time.

The floor of the houses are constructed of split
bamboo braced loosely together, so that it is
possible to see through them, but rather difficult
to walk upon, as they sway about and appear very
fragile. The posts, which are the principal sup-

ports of the house, are six in number, and are
either of bamboo or teak; the former should the
man be poor, the latter if he be in more affluent
circumstances. These posts play a very important
part in the house; they are all named, but the
south post holds the most important position; it is
called the Thabyay-teiny, and it is believed to be
the habitation of the especial nat spirit of the
house. It is looked upon with great respect and
reverence, and decorated with leaves, and the dead
are placed beside it while waiting for burial.

To build a house in Burma is even, if possible,
a more tiresome and aggravating operation than
it is in England, as, before commencing to build,
it is thought necessary that the soil which has
been dug up in the foundations should be shown
to a wise man or soothsayer, and he then pro-
nounces whether it will be a lucky spot to erect
a dwelling upon. The next thing to discover is a
lucky day and hour for commencing operations,
and the third and most burning question of all is
the choice of the posts; these are masculine,
feminine, and neuter. The male posts are those
which are of the same measurement at both ends;
the feminine posts are larger at the base, and the
neuter ones are largest in the centre. There is
also another post called "teing becloo" or ogre post,
and that is very large at the top. It is a general
belief among the Burmans that a house con-

structed with neuter posts will bring misfortune,
and should ogre posts be used death and dire
trouble will attend. Male posts appear to have no
distinct attributes, either for good or evil, so that
they can be used with impunity; but the female
post is the much coveted one, as a house constructed with these brings great happiness and
good fortune to the inmates. But again it may
happen that something in the soil may upset all
these theories and calculations, so that before
finally deciding upon the timbers, it is necessary
once more to seek the aid of a soothsayer; therefore, to erect a house in Burma is a work not to
be lightly undertaken, and one which is calculated
to turn your hair grey, and your temper sour,
before you are fortunate enough to find lucky
posts, a lucky piece of ground, and a lucky day
upon which to commence operations. The roofs
of these dwellings are occasionally made with
small flat tiles, but thatch is more commonly used.
This thatch is generally composed of "danee,"
the leaves of the Toddy Palm, which are soaked
in salt and water to prevent insects from destroy-
ing it. This mode of covering for your house is
no doubt an excellent protection against wet, cold,
and heat; but it has one terrible drawback, viz.,
its very inflammable properties. Fire is a most
terrible scourge in Burma; the houses being of
such very ignitable fabric, and being also very dry,

the least spark sets them into a blaze, which is
most difficult to extinguish, and which generally
ends in the demolition of the whole village. These
constant fires are taken with curious placidness by
the inhabitants.

There are many amusing stories told of the cool,
not to say indifferent manner that a Burman treats
the loss of his house; instead of bewailing the

A MANDALAY CART.

misfortune he gets up a Pwè on the charred
embers, and entirely consoles himself with his
favourite pastime. For the protection of fire each
house has standing outside two long poles, one
called a "Mee-cheht," which is a hooked bamboo
to pull away the thatch; the other is called a
"Meekat," which rather resembles a gridiron,
made of bamboo, and this is used to beat out
the flames.

9

The Burman's house is raised on piles above the ground about seven or eight feet in height, and the space underneath the house is often used as a stable for a horse or cow, should the inhabitants be fortunate enough to possess one ; the accommodation of the house is not large, they generally consist of two or three rooms and a verandah, which is usually three or four feet lower than the level of the other rooms, and is always quite open to the street or garden. The simplicity of the furniture is quite ascetic in quality and quantity. It consists generally of a few woven mats and hard bamboo pillows and a teak box, and if the inhabitants are very advanced, a chair or two. The cooking arrangements and utensils are all of a most primitive description.

The first is a stove constructed out of a box filled with ashes, and wood piled on the top, which, however, answers admirably for boiling rice, which is the staple food of a Burman. The utensils are equally elementary, as they consist of a few earthen pots with lids and a rude kind of spoon with which to stir the contents. The meals are served in a large lacquered bowl (a byat), in which a mass of rice is heaped up, and the curry is doled out in charming little china bowls. Outside, the house has often a small enclosure where they grow sugar-cane, and keep the carts or plough, and where the inevitable rice-mill puts in an appearance. These rice-mills are very primitive inventions. They are constructed of two cylinders hewn out of wood, these are generally about two feet in thickness, and the inner surfaces are made rough. The upper cylinder has an aperture to allow the rice to fall through, and this is worked backwards and forwards by means of a pole, which is attached loosely to it, and the rice comes from between the two cylinders and falls on mats below.

The rice has still to go through another process before it is ready for cooking ; the inner skin or film has to be removed, and this is effected by a kind of " see-saw " arrangement, which acts as a pestle and mortar. It is a thick log balanced on a lever, with a stump of wood let in at one end, and this is often worked by one of the charming Burmese damsels, who stand upon the end and swing up and down, chattering and laughing all the time most gleefully.

One of the most picturesque sights at Mandalay is the silk bazaar. It is the most fascinating study of colour imaginable. There sit rows of bewitching little girls in their brilliant-hued tamehns, all smoking enormous cheroots, while spread out before them lay masses of gorgeous hued silks. These they strive to inveigle the customers to buy, not that it requires much tempting to purchase the Burman silks, which are lovely, both in colour and texture ; they are soft,

and yet they have more body and stiffness than
the Chinese or Japanese.

A certain amount of silk is grown in Burma,
but it is of a coarser quality than that which
comes from China; whether this is occasioned by
its treatment or by the different species of worm
I am unable to say. The people who keep and
tend the silkworms are looked upon very much in
the light of the pagoda slaves, as outcasts, and
altogether unfit company for respectable people
to consort with, and for this reason they generally
dwell quite separately in villages by themselves.
The feeling of horror that they produce upon the
very orthodox Buddhist is inspired by their voca-
tion, which necessitates the constant taking of
life, which is looked upon by the Buddhist religion
with great disfavour ; and all trades, such as
fisheries, &c., which have to do with the destroy-
ing of life, is much discountenanced by Buddha,
and it is supposed that these poor people will have
a most uncomfortable and unenviable lot in the
world to come—all sorts of horrors being in preparation for them as a punishment for their sin.
But in spite of this there are still found people
willing enough to follow the profession and bear
the consequences ; so one concludes that it must
be a paying one to induce them to trifle thus
with their chance of salvation or Nirvana.   The
majority of these silk growers make their habi-

tation on the hillsides, and some of them, besides growing silk, cultivate a little rice by the toung-ya system of clearing the forest and burning the wood.

Like the cultivation of rice in the plains, the silk growing is a very easy matter. Most of us as children went through the craze of keeping silk-

AN UP-COUNTRY CART.

worms and know well the look of the soft yellow cocoons, which were, in our delightful childish imagination, to unwind for us such fascinating yards of silk—silk which in most cases proved phantom silk that never was unwound! But with the Burmans that is different, a great deal is produced and to some purpose. The process is not an arduous or a difficult one, probably if it were either, it would not be practised by a Burman! The silkworms are fed upon the historic mulberry tree and upon leaves of hill shrubs : one of the reasons that most of the silk growers inhabit the hills is because the mulberry trees will not grow or flourish well on the plains, and therefore they live where they can most easily procure food for the worms.

There are many ideas as to how the mulberry tree and the silkworms found their way to Burma as neither of them, it is believed, were natives of the country, though they seem to have taken fairly kindly to the land of their adoption. By some it is said that the art came originally from China and that the Shans were the first to learn it, and that they initiated the Karens and so it was passed on and filtered through to the Burmese. It is most probable that the first idea was originally brought from the Chinese, but whether the Shans or Karens taught the Burmans, or that they learnt it straight from the Chinese is a mystery.

The production of silk, and the manner that it is treated, is of the most simple and primitive description and does not, one would imagine, require a very great brain development. The caterpillars have to be fed, and beyond that there is nothing else of great importance to be done. The lady moths are kept in trays upon some kind of coarse material, and the eggs then adhere to the rough stuff and are thus easily collected, and are then transferred and kept in separate trays. When the baby caterpillars make their appearance they are fed on the best and daintiest leaves that can be procured, but after a few days they change their coats, and then very little attention is paid to them; they, in fact, bring themselves up, and being luckily of a robust and hardy constitution they live, flourish, and let us hope enjoy life.

It takes about three to four weeks before the caterpillar is full grown, and then he begins to do his work in life and spins his cocoon, which he fastens round a strip of bamboo placed in the tray for that purpose. These are after a day or two detached from the bamboo strip and placed in a vessel containing water, which is made to simmer gently over the fire; above the vessel is hung a bamboo reel, upon which the silk is wound, and the winder (who is generally of the fair sex, their fingers being more adapted for this very niggling work), by the aid of a kind of bamboo fork, deftly finds and brings out of the pot the floating ends of silk, and these she winds over the reel, and then passes them on to a cylinder which is placed near to the vessel and to which they are attached, and when this has been effected

she turns the handle of the cylinder and winds on
the silk. It must require a great deal of patience
and neat handling to catch the multiplication of
ends, and when caught not to allow them to
escape or get entangled or broken, which one

BURMESE GIRLS WEAVING WITH A HAND-LOOM.

would imagine must always be happening. No
very great care is taken to keep the silk clean or
in any way to wash it, that is not thought of sufficient consequence. The native silk is used
entirely in the country and sold to those who have
looms, which many houses possess, who spin it up

into clothing. The finer silks and more elaborate
patterns are generally spun from silk procured
from China, but this silk usually comes in quite
a raw condition, and has to go through a rough
preparation, the pieces being twisted into threads
over a wheel, and then boiled in soap and water,
after which process they are considered ready for
dyeing. The dyes are made from seeds, flowers, or
leaves, and sometimes from bark. I believe that
the Jack-tree (*Artocarpus integrifolia*) produces a
very good yellow shade. The colours, I should
say, most affected by the Burmese were pink,
yellow, and green, but I saw very little blue, and
not a great deal of red.

The hand looms which you see many of, and
of which I give a picture, much resemble the old
hand-looms which were used in England some
years back. It is rather fascinating to watch the
silk in these looms growing into some charming
patterned fabric, especially when this is done, as
is nearly always the case, by a charming little
Burmese girl; they handle the loom very deftly,
and make a very attractive picture. At Tsembo
we watched a dear little girl at work for some
time. She was supposed to be the belle of the
place, and we were therefore taken to look at her.
However, she was very much more bashful than
most of the Burmese young ladies, and did not
meet our advances with as much aplomb and kind-

ness as was generally the case, so we retired
feeling rather crushed and sad. Some of the
patterns of the tamehns are very magnificent, and
those which have a design worked in silver are
really gorgeous. One of the most popular patterns
among the ladies is, I believe, called the dog-tooth
pattern ; it is generally composed of orange, green,
and red, and the colours are distributed in a kind
of zigzag pattern, with very much the same idea
of arrangement as the old Italian Punt-Unghero.
I believe that the fashion changes very much in
Burma as regards these patterns, and that a smart
young Burman is quite as particular about the
design of his pasoh as a European masher is about
the exact cut of his coat! When I was in Burma
I should say that large cheques seemed the most
chic things to wear, as the smartest young men
seemed mostly to affect them.

The Burmese girl loves to bargain, be it over the
silks or any other article ; it is more perhaps for
the actual fun and frolic of it than for anything
else. She would be direfully disappointed if you
took the goods at her price, and did not give her
the opportunity of having a really good haggle over
them. She conducts her bargainings admirably,
laughing, gesticulating, and wheedling by turns,
with amusing little shrugs of her shoulders, and
pathetic glances from her brown eyes, until, if
you happen to be a trifle soft-hearted and easily

moved, you find yourself at the end of a very few minutes the happy and enviable possessor of enough silks in which to array your whole family for the next ten years! I spent many happy, but expensive, half hours wandering about the silk bazaar, buying from the fascinating little ladies, and watching the constant and ever-changing panorama of the brilliantly coloured crowd. Every nationality appeared to invest the bazaar; Shans with their great flopping hats and ugly uncouth faces, Chinamen of course, Jews, all mixed with the endless stream of lovely Burmese, who were by far the most interesting of the community.

In a shady corner a couple lingered flirting over the counter of a small stall, and in another a group were laughing over some excellent joke, or bargaining with an energy that became almost alarming, while in a third a company of maidens were gathered together smoking with indolent ease, and putting a few coquettish touches to the flowers in their hair, or the powder on their faces. In every direction that you turned your gaze, a picture full of intense glowing colour was presented to you. I longed to engrave it all upon my mind, to keep it in the picture storehouse of my memory, to be brought out as a gleam of sunshine on some dismal dark day in England. I strove to add to that memory by photography, but perhaps the least said about those photographs the better. They are among the great sorrows of my life! and must be handled tenderly.

I had been foolish enough before starting from Calcutta to purchase a kodak; I do not of course mean for a moment to imply that a kodak necessarily means foolishness! I only wish to advise those who are desirous of having photographs to abstain from buying a kodak in Calcutta, otherwise their tale may be as full of woe and pathos as mine is. I started joyfully off to Burma with the fond belief that I was going to make a most valuable collection of pictures. I photographed everything that came under my gaze, quite regardless of the sun being on the object or not; that was an insignificant detail that I thought quite beneath my notice! I levelled my kodak at everything that took my fancy, touched the button, and concluded that all was completed.

One of these interesting pictures was in the bazaar at Mandalay, and represented three charming young Burmans, evidently quite the *jeunesse dorė* of the town, who were walking jauntily along, and whom I boldly waylaid, and inveigled into standing for their pictures; they were nothing loth, especially when informed that it was to go to London. Alas! for that picture and many others. Whether the climate affected the internal arrangements of that miserable kodak, or whether my workmanship had something to do with it, the result was the same: out of all that army of pictures only five remained to tell the tale; the rest were all taken on one plate—compound photographs, like Mr. Francis Galton's murderers.

We were kindly taken over the prison at Mandalay by the head of it—a charming Parsee doctor. The prisoners do all kinds of trades, and their carving in teak wood is extremely good. Many Dacoits were pointed out to us, and personally I hardly appreciated being locked in with the very worst characters, as we were carefully informed, attended only by two warders, one of which was a prisoner. But the discipline is so admirable that they assured me there was no danger.

CHAPTER VI.

BY far the most interesting relic of the past at Mandalay is the Palace. It is a most curious, quaint structure, and stood originally in the centre of what was called the Royal City. It was surrounded by three high brick walls, only one of which now remains, the Royal City and bazaar being within the outer wall. The ministers and all who possessed high positions resided within the Royal City close to the Palace. Round the outer wall of the city lies a wide moat, which is crossed by several bridges. There were originally twelve gates to the city, each of which was surmounted by a lovely airy structure of pagoda-like roofs; many of these remain, and stand out in charming relief against the blue sky, and break the dull monotony of the long brick wall, and throw delicate, dream-like reflections in the moat beneath.

The space within the walls was in King Thebaw's

THE PALACE, MANDALAY.

time crowded with a mass of buildings, but since our annexation these have been cleared away, and the ground is now relegated to cantonments, and most hideous (though doubtless excellent) barracks.

Lying close round the Palace on the southern side are the remains of a very quaint garden; groves of palms and bananas group themselves in charming distinct companies, and a multiplicity of bridges span a series of wondrous little waterways. Long flights of steps wind up to curious summer-houses, where doubtless the queen and her maidens passed many sunny hours, and where, perchance, under the moonlight's rays sundry tender scenes have oftentimes been enacted.

It is all intensely picturesque, though with a certain childish foolishness. But it is a foolishness that one forgives, and as one wanders to and fro, and dreams of all the bygone greatness, one cannot repress a sigh as one gazes on all the decay which is laying its hand upon every object, and one longs that some effort could be made to preserve this quaint little record of the past.

The Palace itself is a most unique structure. It is built entirely of teak wood, which is carved in the most profuse and elaborate manner with curious patterns and grotesque creatures. It is entirely covered with gilding, excepting where the decoration bursts into an even more florid style,

which takes the form of high dadoes, and doors
constructed of zinc, which are lavishly inlaid with

GARDEN ON SOUTHERN SIDE OF THE PALACE.

fragments of mirror and coloured glass. The
roofs are a very peculiar feature. They are gently
curved, and overhang with deep eaves, and the

matchboard is profusely carved and gilded. Over
the king and queen's apartments these roofs rise
up in many airy tiers, each roof being supported by
delicate pillars, as the higher a person's rank in
society the more roofs he was permitted to have
over his head. Gathered round the actual palace
there are many smaller houses. These were
formerly inhabited by the lesser wives of King
Mindohn-Min, the royal princesses, and maids of
honour to Queen Soo-Paya-Lat; and besides these
smaller abodes a tall pagoda-like spire rears its
gilded and looking-glass-decked head high above
the other picturesque roofs.

The effect of the whole group of buildings is
curiously striking, and would seem the exact type
to attract an Oriental fancy, with their brilliant
lavishness of gilding and colour.

Within, the Palace must have been equally
gorgeous, but it has, alas! been sadly defaced
and spoilt by many of the beautiful council
chambers, halls, &c., being now used for Government offices, which no doubt is in some ways an
excellent use for them, but hardly tends to their
preservation. One of the most beautiful halls has
been turned into a church. It makes a lovely
edifice, but it produces a strange, confused sensa-
tion in one's mind. The Christian service, the
old liturgy and hymns, rising up from this half
grotesque, barbaric building, give one a curious,

bewildering feeling. Another part of these buildings, called the Queen's Hall, which is in by far
the best preservation, has been relegated to the use
of a club, and it certainly makes a most delightful
one. It is absolutely fairy-like in design and ornamentation. The Council Hall, which is used for
a reading-room, is richly decorated with gilding
and carving, and is supported by the most magnificent teak gilded pillars. The dining-room is
very florid in design; it has a high dado of zinc
inlaid with pieces of mirror and coloured glass,
which gives it a little the appearance of a Paris
restaurant. This club is an immense acquisition,
and owing to the great kindness of our Deputy
Commissioner, Mr. Bridge, we passed many pleasant hours there.

In form and proportions these endless halls,
council chambers, &c., are all gracefully conceived,
and, taken as a whole, they present a marvellously
effective picture. Rocco, florid perchance, they
might be dubbed, and yet, look on them when the
soft twilight shadows are laying kindly, shroud-
like hands over the too gaudy parts; look on
them when the sun leaves parting shafts of light
on the glittering mirror-studded spire of the
pagoda, or gently outlines the quaint, carved
eaves, and makes luminous the stately teak
pillars—see them thus, and the memory of them
will linger long, and you will feel that they possess

a dreamy, mystic beauty which bears one back to
the childish delights of fairy-land.

There is another small edifice standing a little
apart from the other group of buildings, which

A BURMESE SOLDIER IN KING THEBAW'S TIME.

possesses a unique grace and charm of its own—
the Looking-glass Monastery erected by King
Mindohn-Min. It is entirely constructed of small

pieces of mirror and coloured glass inlaid in zinc, which is executed with infinite skill and neatness. It is very picturesque in form, and in the sunlight it glitters and scintillates like a myriad gems. It is utterly childish and a little tawdry, and yet, like all this company of buildings, it has a romantic attraction that you cannot explain.

Comparison with other architecture is impossible; these buildings possess a distinct character of their own, and in a way they partake of the nature of the people. Bright, airy, fantastic, glowing with colour and imagination, and in their undurability they also steal something from their constructors, for they are flimsy fabrics, which last but for a space, and have no deep foundations.

A certain sadness appears to linger round these fanciful erections, perchance it is the sorrows of all who suffered there which still seem to haunt the place. Gay and brilliant as the pageant must have been in Thebaw's time, yet the horrors and cruelties perpetrated there have left ghosts that grin and jabber of all those gruesome details.

Queen Soo-Paya-Lat must (if half that is related be true) have bidden fair to rival the great Catherine de Medici in her utter unscrupulousness and barbarity to those who crossed her will, or in any way came beneath her displeasure. She was fiercely jealous, and determined that Thebaw should possess no other legal wife but

THE PALACE.

herself, and in this she was successful, as he was,
I believe, the solitary instance of a King of Burma
who had but one rightful spouse, the number of
the other and less legal ones it would be vain to
count! But these ladies had a perilous time should
the queen have gathered scent of them; woebetide
the luckless damsel who attracted Thebaw's eyes.
She did not often make her appearance again.
The queen "desired to behold her no more,"
which was tantamount to a death sentence; it
was even whispered that the queen had been
known to do the deed herself.

    One very tragic little tale was told to me by an
Armenian lady (Mrs. Manook), whose acquaintance
I had the good fortune to make through Mr.
Smeaton's kindness. Mrs. Manook had held the
scarcely enviable position of lady-in-waiting to
Queen Soo-Paya-Lat, her father, like many other
foreigners, having held a high official office at the
Court. "King Thebaw had been much *épris* with
a very charming and pretty girl, and had doubtless
allowed his admiration to be more apparent than
was at all wise. The queen, ever quick to note
anything of that kind, sent immediately for the
head of the police, and instructed him the course
to be pursued, viz., that she did not wish to see
the girl again. The king, hearing this (though
too cowardly and too much repressed by his consort to dare to interfere openly in her will),

whispered to the official as he withdrew, that he
was to hide the girl, and not put her to death.
This the head of the police did in his own
house for the space of a year, when, as ill luck
would have it, he was despatched upon some
mission, and during his absence the queen, discovering that the wretched girl still lived, had her
taken and killed." Life at the Palace could not
have suffered from any lack of excitement. It
resembled living on a volcano, as you carried your
life in your hand, and were never certain of it for
an hour together. Mrs. Manook told me that
people constantly disappeared, and to my inquiry,
"Did you not ask what became of them?" she
replied, "It was wiser and safer not to notice
their absence." The queen was as fickle as an
April day; one moment she adored a person and
heaped them with favours and presents, while
the next it was quite on the cards that she
desired to see them no more. She had a curious
craze for European articles, and she used to
send to Paris for hundreds of boxes of bonbons, which she distributed among her favourites
or with which she played all kinds of childish
pranks and games. At the birth of her first child
she had an English nurse, and all the baby linen
came from Paris! This is a circumstance worthy
of note, as to the Burman's superstitious nature it
is considered most unlucky to prepare the clothing

for an unborn child. Like all Burmans Soo-Paya-
Lat was intensely fond of amusement ; besides
having constant Pwès, she had every night at the
Palace what is called a Ah Nya, which consisted
of four or five instruments of music, and many
dancing girls.

The arbitrariness and cruelty that existed quite
beggars all description, and the amount of relatives
who were massacred would be hard to enumerate,
while many others were still awaiting their doom
when we (mercifully for them) entered Mandalay.
The mode of killing the princesses was peculiarly
revolting. They beat them on the throat until
they were dead, or nearly so, and then they were
placed in a velvet bag and thrown into the moat
which surrounded the city. This barbarous mode
of dealing with them was on account of its not
being permitted to shed any drop of the blood of a
royal princess.

Mrs. Manook kindly took me to see one of the
few surviving sisters of Thebaw. The poor thing
had been awaiting her doom when we entered
Mandalay and released her with many others. She
is now married to a poor but respectable man in
Mandalay, and receives a small pension from the
Government. She lived in a very poor little native
house, with nothing to distinguish it from its
fellows. She had been considered a beauty, and
there was still a certain grace about her. We sat

near her upon bamboo mats and conversed through
the kind medium of my friend Mrs. Manook. The
princess asked me a great many questions concerning my home and family, and kept inquiring if I
had not been very much alarmed to come so many
thousand miles over the sea. That seemed the
one idea which struck her most strongly in regard
to me. At leaving she presented me with some
enormous cheroots, which I begged to be excused
from smoking, as they measured eleven inches
long and one inch in diameter! A thing that
struck me as very peculiar in Burma was that
no Burman of any position ever lighted his own
cheroot. That office was always performed for
him, the servant puffing vigorously away until the
cheroot was started, when he handed it with great
deference to his master.

Mr. Bridge kindly took us to call upon a
charming old man who had been head of the police
in Thebaw's time, and curiously he was the very
man who had hidden the poor girl whose story
I related above. He was a most courteous and
extremely intelligent old gentleman, and he begged
Mr. Bridge to inform us that had he known of our
intended visit to Mandalay, he would have put one
of his houses (as he possessed two) at our disposal.
His own house was of course like all the other
native dwellings, built of bamboo, and raised some
ten to twelve feet on piles. Its furniture was more

ample than that in the princess's house, as we were given chairs, our host also sitting in one.

Mr. Bridge asked him if he would show us his old robes of office which he used to wear, and which were most gorgeous. He appeared quite pleased at this request, and sent his servant bustling about to various cupboards, and in a few moments some marvellous garments made their appearance. He then inquired if we would like to see him arrayed in them, to which we, of course, assented, and he began to robe himself with the aid of the servant. It was a most amusing sight, the old man eagerly donning his finery, and touching the gorgeous materials with childish delight. At length he was arrayed, and a truly marvellous apparition he presented. The robes of office were most striking and magnificent. They consisted of a pink silk pasoh embroidered in silver, which was tucked up so as to form very loose baggy trousers. A large crimson velvet coat absolutely covered with massive gold lace and a multitude of spangles, and a collar of amazing proportions entirely composed of gold and spangles, and cut out in large peaks which stood out far beyond his shoulders, like a kind of exaggerated Queen Elizabeth's frill, while surmounting all this splendour was the most extraordinary erection upon his head that I have ever beheld. It very much resembled a child's toy gold round helmet, and this was trimmed with a variety of gold and silver frills, while at the top of the extraordinary structure was a tiny golden "Htee" or umbrella,

THE MINISTER OF POLICE IN KING THEBAW'S TIME.

like those which are placed upon the top of a pagoda.

The effect was most grotesque. He looked as if he had just stepped out of the past, from off the stage of some early drama. These were his military

PORTION OF THE INCOMPARABLE PAGODA.

robes of office. The photograph represents him in his ministerial dress.

There was something very touching in the pride which he had in the old dress, and the half-loving manner that he handled it, and the way in which he told us of the things which had been. He allowed that our Government was a most just one, and he takes a great interest in any new developments, and what especially delights him is to accompany Mr. Bridge on some of his expeditions into the district. But with all his friendly feeling towards us, you could see that in his heart he still clung to what was gone, and that to him "old things are best." He misses many things, but perhaps nothing so much as the loss of pageant and colour, which must, and ever will, be so vastly important in an Eastern's life.

An amusing story was told us in regard to this old man. One day Thebaw conceived the idea of abolishing capital punishment, and suggested this to our old friend, upon which he instantly set off to the prison and there ordered about fifty of the prisoners to be executed at once, as he thought he had better make hay while the sun shone, and have one last innings before such a law was passed!

There are endless pagodas at Mandalay, but the most exquisite one, called the Incomparable (in consequence of its marvellous beauty), was, alas, destroyed by fire some few years back.

11

It was not built in the usual conical form, but was a splendid building of magnificent proportions, supported by rows of stately gilded teak pillars. It was a blaze of colour, and decorated in the richest possible manner with carvings and embroideries of the most gorgeous description.

The Arakan Pagoda, which is still in good preservation, has a certain interest attached to it from the great statue of Buddha which it encloses. There is a curious legend told concerning the history of this statue.

During the reign of King Bhodaw-pa-zal the image of Buddha was brought by his eldest son the heir apparent to Amarapura. This image is looked upon as the most sacred of all images, and it is worshipped by the whole of the Buddhist population because it is believed to be the very likeness and image of Buddha himself. The history of the image is the following: "Before Buddha died the people besought him to have an image made in his likeness that he might leave with them to worship after his death. Buddha approved of their request and ordered them to collect every kind of metal that they could find, of which to construct the image. When the image was completed and moulded in the very likeness of Buddha, the head could not be joined to the body. They strove in every possible way to connect it, but all in vain; it always cracked and became detached. Buddha

then came to their aid, and embraced the image
by touching its breast with his own seven times,
and after this the head of the image was joined
without more difficulty. He told the people that
he had inserted his breath into the image, and that
they must hold it ever after in the greatest respect,
and worship the image as his representative after
his death in the same fervent and devout manner
that they worshipped him during his lifetime. By
so doing they would live a long and prosperous
life in this world, and in the next obtain 'Nirvana.'

"Buddha instructed the image neither to speak
nor to preach, but to remain for ever silent, for
he said 'the people would surely come and put
many hard questions, and trouble him with endless
petitions and inquiries. So since that time the
image has not uttered, but been absolutely silent.'"
In Buddha's time it is firmly believed by the
people that the image really conversed with him.

The morning that we went to the Arakan
Pagoda there were crowds of worshippers round
the Great Image, all bearing some small offerings,
and all gazing with the utmost fervour and
devotion upon the great statue.

One of the most unique pagodas, and one which
possesses a charm to which nothing can compare,
is the Cown Mhe Daw, or the 777 pagodas. They
present a most quaint appearance. In the centre is a
small conical-shaped golden pagoda, while gathered

round in symmetrical lines, so as to form a huge square, are this enormous white company of 777 shrines; each of these shrines encloses a verse inscribed upon a kind of tombstone from the Bёetaghats or Buddhist Bible. Not very far removed from these shrines, near the foot of the Mandalay Hills, is the Kyouck Saw Gee, or colossal

THE COWN MHE DAW.

statue of Buddha. It is said to measure twenty-five feet in height, and weighs something enormous. It is enclosed in a rough brick structure, and cannot be said to have any particular beauty, though the rearing of so huge a mass must have been cleverly executed, considering the very primitive appliances that the Burmans then possessed.

By far the most beautiful structure next to the

THE QUEEN'S MONASTERY, MANDALAY.

Palace at Mandalay is the queen's monastery. It was looked upon as a great work of merit to erect one of these havens for monks, and every royal person built one, often more, which they were supposed to support. What is called the queen's golden koung or monastery is a most exquisite building. It is constructed entirely of teak wood, gilded and carved with the most astounding minuteness and elaboration. The roofs, like those of the Palace, are gently curved, and rise in airy, delicate outlines. The Pohn-gyees in their yellow robes, issuing out or standing under the palms near their lovely home, complete a most attractive and unforgetable picture.

CHAPTER VII.

THE journey from Mandalay to Tsembo through the defiles of the Irrawaddy, is one of the most attractive and fascinating tours imaginable.

On Monday, the 25th of February, we embarked on the *Momein*, one of the splendid Irrawaddy Flotilla Company's steamers. These boats are excellent, not to say luxurious; and they have plied the Irrawaddy for many years previous to the annexation of Upper Burma, and both before the war and during it, their officers had several very narrow escapes. One of the captains, a very well-known and respected servant of the company, in his zeal for performing his duties, continued to trade high up the river at the time that the country was most disaffected. He was at length taken prisoner and retained in captivity for some little time, and was actually brought out more than once for execution; but, mercifully, the Burmans' hearts failed

them at the last moment, or their fear of the
English wrath predominated, so that Captain Red-
man, happily, still survives, and commands his
ship on the Irrawaddy.

The country lying immediately round Mandalay
on the northern side has nothing especially attractive or striking about it with the exception of the

MINGOHN PAGODA.

Mandalay Hills, which are charming in outline
and colouring, and which are made even more
picturesque by the innumerable little pagodas with
which they are decked. These quaint little shrines
spring up and peep out on every part of the hillsides.
Some glittering in their golden splendour, others
mere spots of pure white. Most of these shrines
are in different stages of decay, but their ruined

condition rather adds to than detracts from their picturesqueness.

About an hour after leaving Mandalay we passed Mingoon, where close to the river bank is the largest piece of absolutely solid masonry in existence, the gigantic Mingohn Payah (pagoda). This extraordinary structure covers a space of some 450 feet, and its height is 155 feet. It was planned and commenced by King Mintaya Gyee; but, unfortunately, like many other people, both before and since, he did not first sit down and calculate the cost of such a vast undertaking, and so after accomplishing a portion of it, the funds were exhausted, and the great pagoda was never completed. An earthquake in 1839 accelerated the ruthless hand of time in the destruction of this extraordinary monument, and has cleaved the masonry apart and left huge gaping fissures, but even the upheaval of Mother Earth has not been able to destroy this mighty building, and there it stands, and probably will stand until the end of time, a fitting monument to man's folly. The relic chamber of this colossal payah is said to be sixty-one and a half feet square, and eleven feet deep; it was divided into several sections, varying in size, each was supposed to be the resting-place of a holy relic presented by the king or courtiers. The innermost compartments were to enclose the most sacred of those relics.

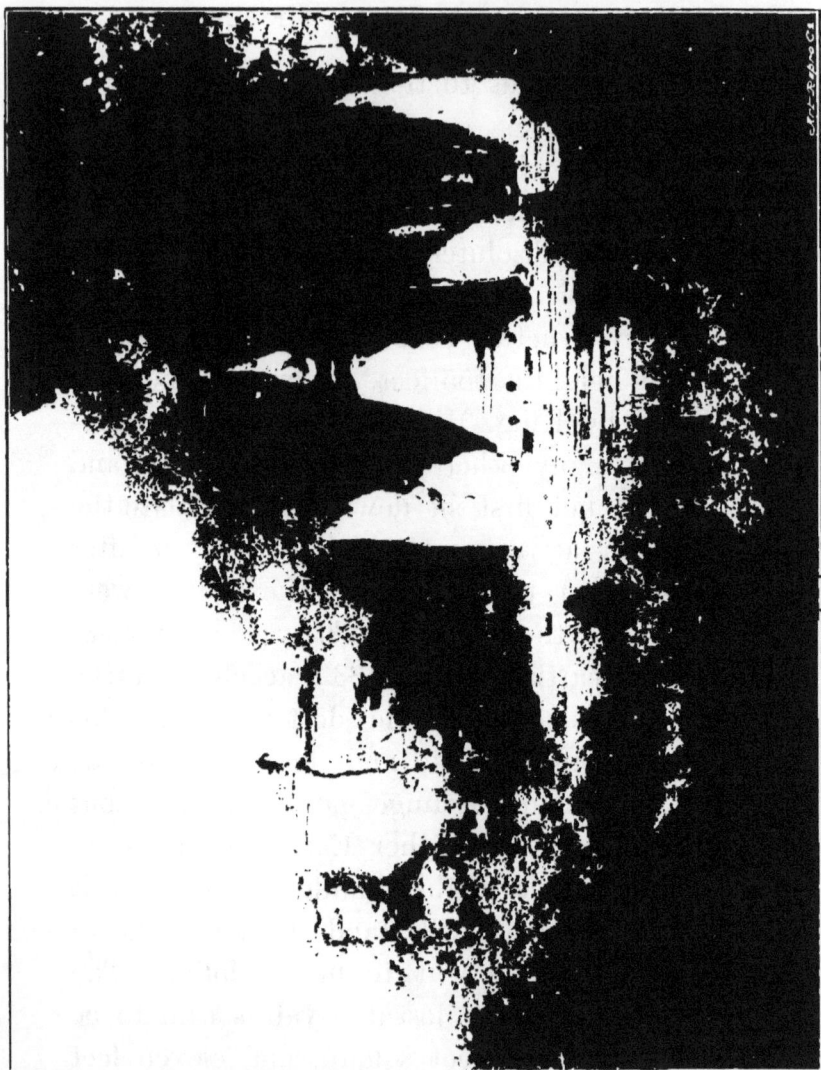

THE GREAT BELL.

The companion to this great pagoda, the enormous bell, is believed to have been cast for it, and it is said to be only second in size to the great bell at Moscow.

The bell now reposes upon the ground, as the wooden staves which held it have long ago rebelled at its unseemly weight. It has a most curious effect resting on the ground, surrounded by a wild, dense jungle. The only habitations near to it being a cluster of bamboo dwellings inhabited by a few nuns who are fed and clothed (as the monks) by the pious population, and who beg a few coins from the very few people who visit these two curious monuments. The Flotilla steamers do not stop at Mingoon on their way up the river, but are very civil in doing so on the return journey should they have passengers on board who desire it.

There is plenty of life on the river between Mandalay and Mingoon, many charming native boats glide swiftly past, and the most picturesque rafts of teak wood, which have come down from Shwegue, float lazily along. Shwegue is a very large depôt for teak wood, and lies high up the river, just before the second defile. Some of the teak-rafts are very large and have quite a village of huts erected upon them, in which the men and their families live. The work of ferrying down the teak-wood is a very congenial one to the Burman. It is not hard work, he can sit in the sun and paddle easily along while he smokes, laughs, talks, and chews betel-nut, and the kindly stream bears him placidly to his destination. The Irrawaddy is at present the great highway of Upper Burma. Nearly all the trade is effected by the steamers, and the population congregate as much as possible near to the river banks.

The first place at which the steamer stops after leaving Mandalay is Kyaukmyaung, a charming little village perched high up on the bank. Many native passengers alighted there, and others embarked. The scene was a most animated one, the boat-load of gaily-dressed natives rowing to the shore, and the stream of villagers pouring down the hill, some come to speed their departing friends, others to gossip and gaze at the big steamer.

Travelling seems to commend itself greatly to the Burman, as the steamer was crowded with native passengers, who were a constant source of delight and amusement to me. I longed to paint them, photograph them, do anything in fact that might in some way perpetuate them, they were so fascinating in their endless variety of costume and race. I used to spend many a half-hour wandering about the deck reserved for the native part of the passengers, watching them and trying by gesticulations to talk to them, to which efforts they responded gladly, shrieking with laughter over our unsuccessful attempts to understand each other. In one corner of the deck sat a group of Chinamen imbibing the well-beloved tea out of delicate Nankin cups, while near to them squatted a joyous company of Burmans, arrayed in gorgeous coloured tamehns and pasohs, talking, laughing, smoking, of course, the longest and fattest of cheroots, and generally gambling with an energy that deserved a better cause.

The game that they mostly affected on board ship was a species of *petits chevaux*, and, unless interrupted by the captain, they would spend hours over it. One of the most curious travelling companions which constantly accompanies a Burman is his cock. Cock-fighting is one of the most treasured pastimes of the Burmese, and though it is practically forbidden by the Government, it is impossible to entirely stamp it out. Besides the Burmese and Chinese there were Jews going up to trade at Bhamo, and Shans, one of the many tribes of Upper Burma. They are a very distinct type from the Burmese, both in appearance and in character. They do not possess their delightful sense of humour, nor their indolent *dolce far niente* nature. They are grave, stolid, and more industrious people, with kindly but ugly faces, which their habit of blacking their teeth does not tend to improve. They have not the Burman's love for brilliant colouring, they dress in sober-hued tamehns, excepting on great occasions, when they don beautifully embroidered petticoats of dark-coloured silk. On their heads they wear a most picturesque kind of dark turban with long ends, and when out in the sun, they substitute these for enormous white straw hats with bright green tassels; these hats flop down on all sides, and give them a most quaint appearance. They have a custom in common with the Burmese, but they carry it to an even more ridiculous extent, viz., boring the most enormous holes in their ears. The lobe of the ear is simply cut out, leaving nothing but a ring of flesh; through these enormous holes the Shans put little rolls of coloured cloth, which cannot be said to be in any way ornamental. The Burmese nearly always wear earrings mounted on large gold cylinders, which fill up these very obnoxious cavities, but should the earrings happen to be absent, they use the holes for a receptacle for any little article, such as cheroots, pens, &c.

After leaving Kyaukmyaung, we passed into the third and lowest defile of the river, and the scenery became most captivating. Glorious wooded banks rose upon both sides of the stream, and many fascinating little native villages were dotted here and there. These picturesque little bamboo structures peeped forth from among thick groves of palms and bananas, while close beside them stood small groups of pagodas which are always the necessary attendants of every Burman village.

The bamboos grew in marvellous profusion, weaving themselves, in parts, into a dense, green wall, while the tamarind, mango, Ficus Religiosa, interspersed with the gorgeous crimson of the Butea Frondosa (or Dak), with occasional Bombax Malabaricum or silk tree, produced an amazing study of colour.

A TEAK RAFT.

We spent the whole afternoon of the 25th in that delightful third defile. Each fresh reach of the river that was disclosed seemed more fascinating than the preceding one. Long stretches of blue, limpid water wandered away, and the brilliant foliage on the banks strayed down to the water's edge and peeped over, as if to gaze at their delicate, wistful reflections in the clear, glittering depths.

12

As we approached Thabyakyin, where we anchored for the night, the hills of the Ruby Mines rose up before us, and made a most attractive feature, lying like a pale blue line in the far distance. Thabyakyin is the station for the Ruby Mines, and it is sixty-one miles west of them. It has, in consequence, become rather an important place, and possesses a Dak bungalow of a kind, and a division of a native regiment. As we had still a short time of daylight left to us after anchoring, we landed and climbed up a very steep sandy bank, upon which a small portion of the village is built, the larger part being along the shore. From the summit of the sandy ridge we had a view of a luxuriant wooded valley, through which the road lies which leads to the much famed Ruby Mines. There are strangely few villages lying between Kyaukmyaung and Thabyakyin. The population appears to be dying out in that part of the country, as there are few appearances of inhabitants, and the captain told us that he had perceived a distinct difference even in the last seven years.

One of the great features on the river are the innumerable little fishermen's huts, which are built close down to the water's edge. These can only be temporary abodes, as in the rains the river rises so enormously, that the banks and any habitations near to them are completely swept

away. At Bhamo large pieces of the banks fall
in, and houses are constantly demolished; but
instead of learning wisdom, and moving farther
inland, the inhabitants still insist on remaining
close to the river (in the same way as the
Neapolitans linger near to Vesuvius). It is so
convenient for watering their cattle, washing
themselves, and fishing, and there is always the
off-chance of the flood not reaching them! The
nets which the fishermen use are rather curious;
they are arranged upon four forks of wood, which
forms a kind of bag; the forks are mounted upon
a primitive lever, so that the net can be raised
or lowered with great facility. They always fish
close to the shore, as the current in mid-stream
is too strong. It must be an isolated, uneventful
life, that of a Burman fisherman. But they are
quite content if they can catch enough fish for
food, sell sufficient to be able to procure wool to
spin into clothing, have a little paddy field, their
beloved cheroots and betel-nut; they desire nothing
more.

The Irrawaddy becomes very low at this season
of the year, and navigation is often extremely
difficult. The deep channel is marked by large
bamboo rods, which are fastened by means of
heavy sand-bags which are sunk in the river
and to which the rods are attached. There is a
very careful system of surveying, otherwise naviga-

tion would be impossible. . It is necessary to observe the greatest precaution, and the steamer is forced to follow a most circuitous route to avoid running upon the many sandy shoals and snags. Two men are sounding the whole time, singing out the depth in quaint, rather melodious voices, and pilots are taken on board at different points. These pilots are nearly always Burmans; they make particularly good pilots, as they have the most wonderful eye for water, and can tell very quickly what is navigable. In spite of all these precautions on our return journey, we were unfortunate enough to run upon one of these hidden snags, which gave the ship a tremendous jar, and ripped up some of the plates; but owing to the splendid exertions of our captain and second officer, this did not delay us, and we arrived at Mandalay quite up to time. These enormous steamers (ours was a three-decker), only draw about four feet of water.

There was very little animal or bird life to be seen upon the river. A few storks and pea-cocks (the Burmese specimens are more beautiful than those of India, having far more gorgeous plumage). A family of monkeys playing in the trees, a flock of paddy birds, a few hawks, a solitary deer come down to the river to drink, and a good many water buffaloes were all that we saw. There are tigers, panthers, and elephants, but they are not very often visible near to the banks of the river. There were originally hippopotamuses, but they have quite disappeared.

We left Thabyakyin at daylight, and after about an hour's steam we issued out of the lovely third defile, and the river became much broader, the hills receded and fell into a low outline, leaving a flat plain and a sandy arid bank. The most interesting feature on that part of the river was the strange old city of Tagoonug, or Tagaung, one of the most ancient capitals of Upper Burma. There are some most curious ruins there, which have been up to the present time very little explored, and their exact history and date are rather shrouded in mystery; but Sir A. P. Phayre, in his history of Burma, says, that "The oldest city, said in Burmese chronicles to have been built by Indian princes, is Tagaung, on the east bank of the Upper Irrawaddy. Colonel Yule is of opinion that it may be identified with the Tugma metropolis of Ptolemy. The existing ruins of Tagaung, so far as they have been explored, give support to the general truth of the tradition as to the seat of the ancient Indo-Burmese monarchy. The Shan people make no claim to heritage in them. Buddhist images and bricks bearing the effigy of Buddha stamped thereon, and Pali inscriptions in ancient devanâgari character, have been found among the ruins. The letters are of the form

referred to the time of the Guptas, used during
the two first centuries of the Christian era. There
appears no good reason for concluding that these
bricks were made at a later period than that
during which similar letters were in use in India.
It has been suggested that the bricks may have
been made at Gayâ, and brought from thence. If
so it would show an early communication between
Upper Burma and Gangetic India. It is, however,
more probable that workmen from India were
brought to make the bricks, or to carve the forms
used to stamp them."

Two hours after passing Tagaung, we came to
a most enchanting little village called Tagine. It
was quite one of the most picturesque of the many
picturesque villages which we had passed. A
great portion of it was built along the shore and
the rest wandered, rather inconsequently, up
the side of a charming little hillside, which was
also decked by a bewitching company of pagodas.
The whole was set in a framework of palms and
bananas, and it possessed a foreground which
would have delighted Tenniers. Crowds of villagers
assembled along the banks, arrayed in every indescribable colour, talking, laughing, and gesticulating, some hurrying on to the steamer, others
hastening off, while a few paddled about in native
dugouts.

These dugouts resemble a small canoe, with a

flat spoon-like stern and bow, upon which two
Burmans squat and paddle in the most cunning
manner; how they ever succeed in keeping their
balance is marvellous, as the space that they sit
upon cannot be more than eleven or twelve inches
in width, but they look perfectly happy, and go
along at a good pace. The country, after leaving

A NATIVE VILLAGE.

Tagine, again became most attractive. Hills
covered with dense forests rose up in different
gradations, and the banks were once more trimmed
with the most luxuriant of foliage, and with long
crimson patches of the glorious Butea Frondosa
(or Dak), among whose dazzling branches occasional herds of grotesque monkeys gamboled and
swung in chattering delight. Now and again the

river widened out until it formed a kind of estuary or lake, which produced a fascinating effect and reminded one slightly of Scotland.

One of the most picturesque of these reaches we passed just at sunset, and the effect was absolutely dreamlike, the reflections in the clear, limpid water quite unimaginable. The deep, though delicate blue of the hills standing out with distinct intentness against a gold burnished sky, the brilliant green of the foliage, all was depicted with the utmost vividness in the translucent waters. It lingered, alas, for all too short a space, and then faded mystically away, leaving the landscape bathed in deep purple haze.

We anchored for the second night mid-stream, a little above the Shoay Lee, one of the tributaries of the Irrawaddy, which rises near to the town of Momein.

On the 27th we were once more under way. We always started at daylight, which meant about six o'clock, and at seven we reached Katha, one of the largest town in Upper Burma. It was not a particularly prepossessing looking place, but it had a certain melancholy interest attached to it, as the Government has lately commenced the construction of a railway there, which is to run north and south, and which is, I believe, at the present time completed. This railway will doubtless be an enormous help in opening up this large tract of country, and of improving its commercial enterprises ; but it was impossible to restrain a deep sigh of regret, that the great iron horse was so soon to trample over this sweet primitive corner of the world, and leave the print of his heavy foot among all this charming simplicity and content.

It is so refreshing in this bustling, hurrying, nineteenth century, to come from the be-railwayed and be-businessed West, and discover one little oasis where Nature is still allowed to rampage at will, and where money is not the one and all-absorbing object of people's lives. But as gold has also lately been found in the neighbourhood of Katha, one fears that this charming Arcadian simplicity will not last long.

About an hour after leaving Katha we stopped at Modah, which struck me as being peculiarly attractive. The pagodas had all gathered themselves together on a small eminence, and gazed down benignly like guardian angels on the trim little village beneath. Shwegue, which was our next halting-place, was decidedly mediocre, but it had the virtue of being one of the largest depôts for teak. Kyoodan, which lies a little farther up the river on the opposite side was simply a bare patch of sand, and there we beheld immense preparations which were being made for a great yearly fair. Whole streets of quaint little tents and booths were being erected upon the sandy

shore, till there was quite a small white city. One
year we were told a great disaster had occurred.
A storm came up just as all was completed and
washed the whole of the little flimsy town away.
It was a most picturesque sight. A perfect fleet
of little native boats was anchored along the
shore, while others plied backwards and forwards,
bearing in them lovely dressed girls and men, who
were evidently on their way to the fair. Many of
them were singing to quaint instruments, and
their voices, laughter, and music filled the air
with delicious melody. Here, alas, we landed
nearly all our native passengers. It was a real
regret to me to see them disembarking. They
made a wondrously lovely group standing together
on the shore, in their glowing coloured silks, and
most picturesque Chinese umbrellas held daintily
over their heads. We waved them a last farewell,
and saw them trudge away to the fair, where
doubtless they were going to have a really
beautiful time!

After leaving Kyoodan we entered the second
defile. It is of an entirely different character
from the first. The first is charming, *riante*, and
sunny; the second is grand, stately, serious. The
river appears to have cleft the mountains asunder,
and winds in and out through a magnificent gorge,
with the gaunt grey cliffs rising up sheer from the
water's edge some two hundred feet. Sharp per-

pendicular rocks and crags stand out, and hang
over the wild abyss beneath, as if they would hurl
themselves down on any unlucky craft below. The
shadows, the stillness, and the green forest-clad
hills hovering above the crags, and the dark, lurid
blue depths of the waters beneath seem to strike
one with a sudden dumb awe; and a half eerie

ENTRANCE TO SECOND DEFILE.

feeling possessed one, till one's eyes fell on a tiny
ray of sunlight, which had crept down from the
mountain tops and lay like a brilliant emerald on
the waving, rustling bamboos, and then wandered
on to the grey crags and rocks, till it left them
arrayed in a robe of sheeny gold.

The second defile is, alas! like all the good
things of this world, of transient duration, and we

issued out all too soon. The river again became
wide, and the shores low and sandy, and the banks
as little interesting as it is possible for anything to
be on the Irrawaddy, where there is always something charming, either in colour, or form, for the
eye to rest upon. We again anchored mid-stream,
and on Thursday morning, the 28th, we arrived at
Bhamo.

CHAPTER VIII.

BHAMO AND TSEMBO.

BHAMO is a long, straggling place—in fact, it is so straggling and disconnected that some of the houses appear to have been left behind altogether, while the others have stalked on so far in front that they seem to have abandoned the rest of the community and left them quite out of sight. This curiously unsociable company of houses meanders along the river bank for a distance of about three miles. In one part the houses appear to be on slightly more friendly terms, and have congregated together forming a very attractive little village street, from which the spires of several pagodas and the quaint airy roofs of a Pohn-gyee koung stand out in picturesque distinctness. There is a small Chinese quarter which stands rather back from the river, and which, with the usual unsociability of Bhamo, appears to have no apparent connection with the rest of the town. Here John Chinaman reigns supreme, and sits at

the receipt of custom in his funny little shop, ready
and willing to trade or gamble with any who will
come.

BHAMO.

Bhamo is a very cosmopolitan place. There are
Burmese, Chinese, Jews, Shans, and Kachins.
The latter are hill people who are a wild, lawless

set, and certainly their looks are not attractive, and
I should most assuredly prefer not meeting one
alone on a dark night in a blind alley! They have
a wild ruggedness of mien and dress, which suggest
unpleasantly the long knife, and the ungovernable
passions of a savage. They have given us a great
deal of trouble, raiding down upon villages and
carrying off cattle and other property, and in many
cases killing and wounding the inhabitants if any
resistance was offered.

While we were in Bhamo they were having a
good deal of difficulty with them at a place about
fifty miles distant. They are difficult people to
catch among their mountain strongholds, and
when caught, extremely unpleasant enemies to
tackle, hiding as they do among the thick jungle,
and potting our soldiers when they themselves are
in comparative safety. They possess the quickness
of cats, and they escape through the dense brushwood long before our men can follow them. The
troops which have been most useful to us in this
guerilla warfare are the Goorkhas; with their
nimbleness, they are quite a match for the Kachins,
and dart into the jungle in pursuit of them, and
finish a good many with their kukri knives.

Besides the Chinese, Burmese, Jews, Shans, and
Kachins, there are Chinese Shans and Burmese
Shans, as they intermarry frequently. As there is
no caste in Burma a Burmese maiden does not in

the least object to a foreign husband; she has no
narrow prejudices of that kind, which in some
ways has great disadvantages, and is to be deplored, as at no very distant date there will be,
it is feared, few pure Burmans remaining.

Bhamo is becoming quite an important place,
and will no doubt go on increasing as the country
beyond is more opened out and developed. At the
present time it has a population of some eight
thousand, a deputy commissioner, and a certain
number of English and native troops.

Bhamo is the great river port and headquarters
of the cotton trade between India and China.
The cotton is brought up to Bhamo by boat, and
is there either forwarded all the way by caravans,
or trans-shipped on to native boats which take it up
the Taping river, at the head of which it is met
and conveyed over the frontier on mules, a duty of
six annas being levied on each load of cotton that
enters China. The caravans which came for the
cotton are a most curious sight; they are composed
of mules, ponies, donkeys, and oxen—the most
extraordinary heterogeneous company of animals
and drovers that can be imagined. They come
from China, which is a distance of some forty
miles, bearing loads of jade stone and wax, and in
return they carry back the cotton. They remain
in Bhamo for a few days to rest and unload and
reload, and while there they encamp themselves on

a large broken piece of ground, lying along the
river bank. They are verily a weird sight, a
motley crew, numbering some hundreds of beasts,
and uncouth, wild-looking attendants. One of
these caravans had just arrived when we were at
Bhamo, and it was a most amusing sight watching
them load up the donkeys, who rebelled vigorously

THE CHINESE QUARTER OF BHAMO.

at the weight of cotton put upon them, often, poor
beasts, in consequence of their backs being scored
by the pack saddles, and the weight doubtless gave
the poor creatures great pain. That, it is needless
to remark, was of no moment to a Chinese drover!
These caravans are not desirable visitors as they
constantly bring in anthrax and other diseases.

13

Bhamo has, beside the cotton, a large trade in orchids, which grow in great profusion in the beautiful first defile of the river between Bhamo and Tsembo. The Burmans collect the plants in December and January, and bring them down to Bhamo, where many buyers from Rangoon and even Calcutta come to purchase them. The market value of an orchid there is about one rupee a plant, or, should they be especially rare specimens, two rupees.

The view from Bhamo is extremely varied; water, mountains, and jungle are spread out before you in charming variety, and delight your eye with their graceful outlines and glowing colours. A luxuriant plain covered with dense jungle stretches away at the back of the town, until it loses itself at the feet of a lovely range of mountains. These mountains are clothed with a phantom-like mist in the early morning and grow a burning, dazzling purple in the evening light. On the opposite side of the town your eye wanders over a wide expanse of waters, as at Bhamo the river widens out considerably, and gives the idea of a large lake, with here and there a sandbank protruding out of its glassy surface, while beyond again another exquisite chain of mountains spans the horizon.

About three miles from Bhamo, buried deep in the jungle, are a curious group of pagodas. In the centre is a large golden one, called the Shway

Gyine, and this is surrounded by many hundreds of satellites. The history and age of this curious company are unknown, but it is imagined by some that they were erected by a Shan chief. There is an absurd legend told in connection with them. " Buddha, during one of his endless incarnations, became a cock, and, during the period of his cock life, it is affirmed that he came and scratched at that spot, hence it became holy, and the pagodas were erected upon it."

We remained on board the steamer during our stay in Bhamo, as at present there is nothing approaching an hotel, and I am uncertain whether there is even a Dak bungalow. We spent several pleasant evenings with our kind friends, Mr. and Mrs. Todd Naylor, he having just assumed the duties of Deputy Commissioner. We had some most amusing rides out to dinner at his house, which lay about two miles away from where the steamer was anchored.

The roads in Bhamo are at present decidedly elementary, and leave a good deal to the imagination, and driving is not altogether easy or pleasant. Mr. Todd Naylor was therefore kind enough to send us down two charming little Burman ponies, which we mounted and rode through the darkness, accompanied by a lantern. It was very interesting riding through the town at night. I was immensely struck by the domestic nature of the inhabitants. As we passed along we saw several charming family groups sitting together in their houses working, laughing, and of course smoking. They appeared to retire to rest at a very early hour, as on our return, which was generally about ten or half-past, there was not a sound, all was enveloped in darkness, and the streets were absolutely deserted, except for the presence of a few pariah dogs.

The Burmese are a wonderfully clean people, and it was very amusing at Bhamo to watch the little girls coming to the river for their bath, which they did every afternoon with great regularity. They sat close down to the water's edge, and poured pail after pail over their graceful little bodies, retaining their tamehns all the time, after which they threw a dry tamehn round them, over the wet one, which, by some cunning arrangement, fell off exactly at the right moment, leaving them attired in a clean, dry garment. After this process they used to wash their hair, the false tails as well as what was growing on their heads. The whole proceeding appeared to give them infinite delight, for there were peals of laughter the whole time.

We remained for one day at Bhamo on our way up to Tsembo, and two days on our return journey. We were not able to proceed to Tsembo by the small Flotilla steamer, which is generally running,

as it had unfortunately run aground near Myitkyna,
a not uncommon occurrence at that season of the
year, when the river is so very low.   It is not alto-

SHAN MAN AND WOMAN.

gether a desirable adventure to befall you, as when
you are stranded on a sandbank, mid-stream, and

in a part of the river far removed from any village,
your provisions have a disagreeable habit of
becoming a little short. The defile which lies
between Bhamo and Tsembo is by far the most
beautiful part of the river, being immeasurably
wilder and grander than any country that we had
passed through. When the Flotilla steamer did
not make her appearance, we began to be rather
disconsolate as that piece of the river was what
we were most desirous of seeing, and our dis-
appointment would have been keen had we not
been able to effect it; but, owing to the kindness
of our friend, Mr. Todd Naylor, we were allowed a
passage upon a Government launch, and we were
kindly brought back by a returning one on the
following day. The steamers which go upon that
part of the river are obliged to be quite small on
account of the great rapidity of the currents and
the extreme narrowness of the passage, which in
places would only allow the navigation of a small
craft. Tsembo lies forty miles distant from
Bhamo, and is at present the great centre where
supplies are sent for transport to the stations
beyond, such as Mogaung and Myitkyna.

We left Bhamo at eight o'clock on the morning
of Friday, the 1st of March. We were some time
in actually getting under way, as our three
fellow passengers took a long time to arrange
themselves. They consisted of a German geolo-

gist, who was on his way up north to prospect
for mines; a German miner, who was accompany-
ing him; and an American Baptist missionary,
who was attending the party in capacity, I
believe, of protector, as he knew and was well
known by the tribes in whose country they were
purposing to travel. It was rather a work of difficulty collecting all their baggage and getting it on
board, the most difficult part of which were two
ponies, who evinced a very strong disposition to
stay on land, and were most vigorous in their
attempt to frustrate all efforts to get them on to the
boat. At last, however, all were embarked—ponies,
missionary, German doctor, servants, and baggage
—and away we started. The only person, I think,
who did not share our delight was the German
doctor, who appeared of a timid disposition, and
did not seem entirely to relish his mission, and I
think he not unfrequently wished himself back in
his beloved Fatherland. He amused us extremely
by his nervousness, and by a habit he had,
whenever the steamer stopped, of sending his
servant on land to chip off pieces of rock. On
one occasion the servant was as nearly as possible
left behind.

The whole forty miles between Bhamo and
Tsembo are marvellously beautiful. The river
winds right through the Burman and Kachin
mountains, where the scenery is simply gorgeous.

At the commencement the banks are flat, but
clothed with every kind of verdure, and sprinkled
with a multitude of dainty villages and pagodas.
As you proceed the banks begin gradually to rise,
and the river narrows and runs straight into the
very heart of the mountains. On all sides these
magnificent hills rise around you, clothed with

THE FIRST DEFILE.

waving bamboo, tamarind, peepul, and mango,
and on many of the trees was festooned in lovely
mauve tresses an exquisite creeper, called, in
Burmese, Panza.

The whole scene was absolutely bewildering;
one looked here and looked there till one's eyes
became satiated with the loveliness around
one.

The shores on each side were most varied,
broken into endless picture-like creeks, bays,
promontories, and islands; while along the edge
giant rocks were piled one upon another, or thrust
up their grey heads in picturesque, though evil,
intent from among the blue swirling stream.

Ever and anon some bewitching little native

NEAR THE ELEPHANT ROCK. FIRST DEFILE.

village and pagoda peeped out high above your
head, on the steep hillside, embowered in rustling
bamboos, and once we were borne past a fascinating little island upon which were deftly placed,
sheltered by graceful foliage, a delicate little company of pagodas. A few native boats were carried
swiftly past us on the rapid stream ladened with

gaily dressed natives, otherwise we saw no life or
boats of any sort upon that part of the river. The
reason is the extreme danger of the currents,
which run with the most astounding force, and
the river winds in the most amazing manner.
At one place, close to what is called the Elephant
rock, it turns at a complete right angle, and the
stream there rushes and tears along at a speed
which is quite terrific, and it requires most careful
steering to pilot the boat safely through. As you
proceed farther up the defile the scenery becomes
more and more beautiful. The hills rise higher
and higher, and the whole scene reminds one of a
tropical Scotland—Scotland with her rippling blue
streams, her grey rocks, and her purple mountains,
but with the glorious vegetation of the East. You
reach the climax of all this transcendent loveliness
at the Pasha Gate, a very narrow gorge, where the
sharp crags hang frowning above your head, and
it would almost seem that they had been cleft
asunder, for the rocks were strewn here and there
in wild confusion, and the hills seem to have
gathered themselves together in close and loving
communion.

The gate itself is formed by huge grey rocks
piled one upon another which rise there out
of the water to a height of some forty or fifty
feet, and rear their jagged edge with cruel distinctness against the brilliant green background.

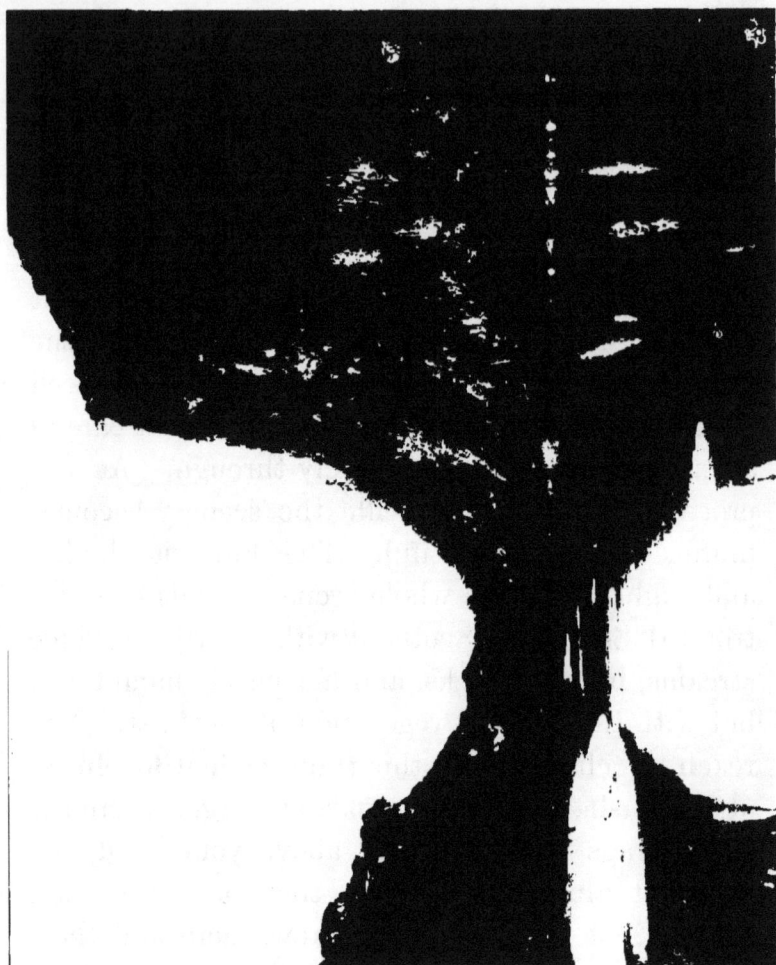

It is a wild, weird spot—a place where Macbeth's witches might have met, or gnomes and evil spirits wandered, when the moon had hidden her face, and only a star peeped down on the black, crowd of rocks, and listened to the dull roar of the mighty waters. The massive crags stand like giant sentinels, who would fain warn the careless how they dare venture past, while the swirling, rushing body of waters eddies and tears through the narrow passage as if it would carry all along in its mighty embrace. The Pasha Gate stands very near to the end of the defile, and after traversing a few more miles of really ideal scenery the passage through the hills is over, and with deep regret you once more issue out into a wide reach with sandbanks again protruding their yellow heads, and in front, on the left bank of the river, Tsembo presents itself to your gaze.

We noticed a goodly company of fishermen, as we issued out of the defile, all fishing with the same kind of net as lower down the river, but without the lever attached to it. There seemed to be a multiplicity of fish, as we saw several of them pull up their nets full of glittering and flopping little denisons of the river. I do not recollect seeing any animal life on that part of the river, with the exception of two otters who were basking in the sun on a sandy shoal, otherwise it seemed deserted, or the jungle was so

dense and impenetrable that it was impossible to
see into it passing, as we were, swiftly along.

Tsembo is a quaint little village perched high
upon the cliff, which is a most necessary precaution, as in the rains the river rises there to a
height of eighty-five feet. When one looks down
on the water below, one can hardly credit the
veracity of this statement, but at the top of the
cliff we were shown a palm tree, and told that
some four or five months previously the steamers
had been tied to that tree. It sounds rather like
the story of Baron Munchausen, who, in the snow,
tied his horse to the steeple of a church, and was
astonished in the morning to find it suspended in
mid-air; but astounding as it may appear, it is
absolutely true that the river actually rises eighty-
five feet at that point. The waters pile themselves
up before the entrance to the defile, and then hurl
themselves through the narrow opening in a surging, roaring torrent.

For about four months of the year that part of
the river is absolutely impassable for steamers, as
the rapidity of the current is simply appalling. A
few native boats go up and down, but it is perilous
work to keep them afloat in the swirling, rushing stream, which flees along with such terrific
impetus.

To give some idea of the great difficulty and
danger in navigating this part of the river, I give

the following accident which happened there to a
friend of mine who went up to Tsembo some two
months before we did. He was on board an Irrawaddy Flotilla steamer, and when they had got
close to the Pasha Gate the current was so fierce
that it carried away a portion of the steering gear,
which left the little boat in a most perilous position, and entirely at the mercy of these awful
currents. The boat spun round and round several
times like a teetotum, most providentially not
coming in its mad race in contact with any of the
rocks, whose ugly faces and sharp outlines protrude
themselves so profusely in that part: the boat then
mercifully drifting near to the shore, some of the
crew jumped over with hawsers and made her fast
in a little bay while they rectified the damage.
But it was a moment of immense danger, as the
narrowness of the river at that point, and with
the perfect walls of rocks which surround it, a
vessel has little or no chance of escape. I was
told that one of the things calculated to shake
the strongest of nerves was a passage down that
part of the river in a *native boat* in *flood* time!
The Burmese are excellent boatmen, but the pace
the little craft is carried over those surging,
swirling waters is something that one remembers
long, and does not in many cases wish to repeat.

There is now a road between Bhamo and
Tsembo. Previously to this Tsembo and the

country beyond were entirely cut off during the rains, excepting for the occasional native boat which managed to get up or down.

We were very kindly received at Tsembo by Mr. Wallace, who was stationed there in charge of the Government steamers which run up and down the river, to Bhamo on the south, and Myitkyna on the north. He most kindly invited us to tea, and escorted us all round the sights of Tsembo, which were not numerous. There were several curious pagodas, and a weird old bell, supported by two carved wooden figures, and a very picturesque Pohn-gyee koung, shaded by some charming peepul trees. As we wandered by this edifice an interesting little ceremony was being performed—the offering of gifts to the Pohn-gyee. A row of charmingly woven rush baskets were placed in front of the shrine filled with rice, vegetables, and fruits. A graceful group of women sat before the holy man, and many of them carried little vases with flowers. It was a fascinating picture. The setting sun streamed in, and illuminated the Pohn-gyee's yellow robes with a sheen of gold, and then strayed on a little farther and crept up on to the tiny shrine and lay tenderly on the women's bent heads. We lingered for several minutes silent spectators, and then as we turned to leave I expressed some admiration for the flowers which the women carried, and they, with their quick perception and ever-courteous wish to give you pleasure, instantly presented them to me. The Pohn-gyee also begged my acceptance of a lovely bunch of yellow bananas, such bananas, indeed, as only Burma can produce.

We had tea with our hospitable friend, Mr. Wallace, who lived in a real Burmese house, with the exception of having a plank floor instead of

TSEMBO.

one constructed only of bamboo. After tea] he suggested that we should go to dinner with him, adding that he hoped we should not mind bringing our own knives and forks and mugs, as he had a very limited supply. This we were, of course, delighted to do, as we had come prepared with all necessaries, as the boat we came on was a mere launch with two little bamboo cabins, which, of

14

course, were quite innocent of any furniture whatever. However, we slept splendidly on the floor, in
a capital bed of rugs and pillows, and performed our
ablutions out of a large zinc pail, and began almost
to think that all the appurtenances and luxuries
of civilisation were a mistake! We had a most
amusing dinner with Mr. Wallace and the American missionary, who had also been invited. The
German doctor was in too agitated a frame of
mind at the perils that he imagined he was going
to face to allow himself such frivolity. After
dinner we wandered down and looked at a Pwè
which was being performed, the music and singing
of which had been going on most vociferously all
through dinner. It was a weird sight, these wild-
looking creatures, dressed, or, rather, in this
instance, not much dressed, whirling round and
round, posturing, acting, shrieking, and placing
themselves in every kind of attitude, not always
the most graceful, while around them were collected
the whole village, encouraging the performance
by occasionally joining in, or with roars of laughter
at some joke which I should imagine was not over-
burdened with refinement. It was certainly most
barbaric, and made one realise that Tsembo was
not exactly in the centre of civilisation. We
parted with our travelling companions on the
following morning, they proceeding to Myitkyna
and then striking up-country, while we reluctantly

bade Mr. Wallace farewell, and retraced our steps on another Government launch back to Bhamo. It took us seven hours to accomplish the distance going up, and only four on our return journey, which will give some idea of the swiftness at which the stream runs even at that season of the year.

CHAPTER IX.

THE marvellous fertility of Burma and the richness of its flora are one of the most striking
and delightful of its many attractions. To those
who are botanists, Burma holds forth a whole
mine of enchantment, while to others who, like
myself, love plants, trees, and flowers for their
beauty of form and colour, but who, alas, only
take an ignorant but keen interest in them, Burma
likewise presents manifold charms. It is a very
curious coincidence that many of the extra-tropical
plants which grow in Burma on the plains are
in India only to be found on mountains or on
quite high elevations, and therefore in a cooler
climate. For instance, I believe that I am correct
in saying that the Pinus longifolia grows in the
Thoung-gyeen Valley, which is only something
like three hundred feet above the sea level, and
the Garcinia pictoria, which as a rule shows
itself only at great heights, is found in Burma at
a quite low elevation.

Among the most beautiful of the ornament trees
is the Amherstia nobilis, which is entirely peculiar
to Burma. It has the most graceful of forms,
with brilliant green foliage and glowing scarlet
flowers, which fall droopingly from exquisite pen-
dulous branches. The flowers partake a little of
the Diclytria, and seem to drape themselves and
hang like great crimson tassels. One of the most
beautiful specimens of this tree that I saw grew in
Mr. Smeaton's garden at Rangoon ; and many is
the hour I have spent peering admiringly into its
cool emerald depths, and letting my eyes feast
on its glorious flowers. A very interesting and
charming little account of it is given by Lieutenant-
General Albert Fytche in his work on Burma, and
I have ventured to quote his account of the tree in
his own words : " The Amherstia was first discovered
near Troela, on the Salween river, by Dr. Wallich,
and named by him after Lady Amherst, the wife of
the then Governor-General of India. Dr. Wallich
says that there can be no doubt that this tree,
when in foliage and blossom, is the most strikingly
superb object which can possibly be imagined. It
is unequalled in the flora of the East. Its precise
habitat was unknown until 1865, when it was discovered by the Rev. C. Parish growing wild on the
banks of the Yoondzaleen river. From the fact
of old trees of this species being found only in
the vicinity of sacred places, it was for a long

time supposed not to be indigenous to Burma, but to have been introduced by Buddhist pilgrims from the Shan States or China. It is often planted in company with the Jonesia, which is called by the Burmese the wife of the Amherstia. The tree first discovered by Dr. Wallich was growing beside a Jonesia ; and the symmetry and numerous graceful raceme of crimson and orange blossoms of the latter well fit it for such companionship.

" According to Klaproth, Gautama was born under this tree ; and within the fall of its shadow, and at the instant of his birth he delivered his first harangue. With a voice that resembled the roaring of a lion he exclaimed, ' I am the most excellent of men. I am the most famous of men. I am the most victorious of men ! ' "

Another interesting and beautiful tree is the Padouk, which is said to blossom three times before the rains, and after the third time the monsoon, it is believed, must break, the flowers only last for a very short space and give out a delicious odour.

One of the flowers which the Burmese damsels mostly affect for the decking of their hair is the Champac (or Michelia Champaca). It has lovely golden-coloured blooms ; but the very strong scent is said by some to entirely deter the bees from visiting it. If this is the case, it would be curious to know how it is fertilised. The Brahmins have a very poetical idea with regard to it, *i.e.*, that there exists a blue variety of this tree, but that it is only possible for it to blossom in Paradise.

Another tree which bids fair to rival those that I have already mentioned is the Mesua. It has the most exquisite alabaster blossoms, with gorgeous yellow stamens, which look as if they had been born in a world so pure and fair that it could have no part with this soiled, tarnished earth of ours. The tree possesses also a very charming power of being able to don its new coat of lovely crimson leaves before discarding its former garments of last year. These flowers are often presented by the Burmese as a New Year's gift, and the tree is also held in great veneration, as it is believed that the coming Buddha Arāmaitriya will make his entrance upon his new life while in meditation under this tree.

Of palms and bamboos there are a goodly company of endless varieties, and the delicate waving foliage add immensely to the beauty of the forests. There are endless species of bamboo, but the Bamboo Gigantia, and, I believe, the Mikati and Nigris grow in the most extraordinary profusion. Of the palms there are the Cocos, Licuala, Livistona, Areca, and many others. The Cocos, Areca, and Borassus Flabelliformis are among those which are most common.

The palm trees are made use of in several ways,

and the leaves of the palmyra are converted into a substitute for paper, some of them being of a great size. The books used by the Pohn-gyees, and all the old sacred Buddhist works were all written upon palm leaves with a very thin steel style. The nut of the Areca catechu is much used by the Burmans to chew, mixed with lime and betel peper. It possesses a very disagreeable power of turning the saliva and teeth red when mastication is taking place, which spoils the appearance of many a dainty little Burmese girl. The palm leaves are also much used for fans, which the Pohn-gyees are supposed to use to shade their eyes from lighting upon any fair damsels! The sap of the palm Corypha Umbraculifera is also converted into a kind of sugar. The female tree curiously produces a great deal more of this sweet juice than the male one has the power of doing.

Of fruits Burma is exceedingly rich. Plantains grow in immense profusion, and the pineapple is cultivated enormously, near to Rangoon, and are marvellously cheap. Mangoes, oranges, citrons, are of course found in great plenitude, also the Dorian, which the Burmese themselves much enjoy. But I fancy that it is a very acquired taste, as it has a curious, not to say unpleasant odour, and Europeans generally told me that it was horrid! The fruit which requires no acquired taste to enjoy is the Mangosteen. These are

peculiar to the Malay Archipelago, and are perfectly delicious, and bid fair to rival a peach, and
to my taste have a far more delicate flavour than
the far-famed mango ; they have also another great
advantage, as they are not as difficult to eat.
Another of the fruit trees of Burma is the Pierardia
Sapota, whose fruit rather resembles grapes in form
and growth.

So much has been written about the glorious
fertility of Burma and the marvellous growth of
trees, creepers, and orchids, that I feel that there
is little left for me to say. But it is impossible
for any one to make a journey up the Irrawaddy
without being amazed and enchanted by the size
and luxuriance of everything that he beholds. The
trees are festooned by gorgeous flowering creepers,
hardly one tree is free from some parasite which
has wound itself round the trunk and crept up
into the branches, where it fain, too, would enjoy
the light and sunshine of God's heaven. Whether
the trees appreciate the close and loving embrace
of these beautiful but probably dangerous admirers
is doubtful; but from a purely artistic point of view,
nothing can be more exquisite and picturesque.

By far the most valuable tree in Burma is the
teak. It is used enormously in the country, and
also exported in great quantities. There are many
varieties, but I believe that the Tectona grandis is
the most important one, and that most used for

export; it reaches its maturity in about eighty years.

It is generally an enormous tree, measuring often in height some fifty to sixty feet, and in girth as much as twelve to fifteen or sixteen feet. It is wood that takes a comparatively short time to season, and it is used enormously by the Burmese for their carvings. In fact, everything practically that is not built of bamboo or brick in Burma, is built of teak wood.

There is another variety which is also exported, but it is darker in colour and possesses a closer grain. The remaining kinds are generally only made use of in the country itself.

The teak grows to the greatest perfection on the high or hill forests; and what is a peculiar feature in regard to it, is that it seldom grows together in very large quantities, being usually found mixed with other trees. It also shows its love for sunshine by growing best on the southern sides of the hills, and its dislike to wind, as on any exposed ridge it becomes extremely scarce. The soil that it seems to approve of most, is a grey, stiff, sandy clay, derived from the slate clay. The foliage of the teak tree had unfortunately nearly departed when we went up the Irrawaddy, but the leaves are of a great size, measuring sometimes as much as ten to eighteen inches in length, and eight to sixteen in breadth. The time that its pale yellow

TEAK RAFTS.

flowers and its verdure is at its best is after the rains. It produces its seeds also at that time, and these seeds are contained in a hard shell which cannot be softened and melted without a great deal of heat and moisture, so that the imprisoned seed has to await its liberation before it can begin to grow; and owing to this, if one might say, tardy invention of nature, the seed loses many valuable weeks before it can begin to propagate itself. But when once it is let loose it makes the best possible use of its time, and certainly seems determined to lose no more hours, as it makes enormous shoots, sometimes as much as the height of eleven to twelve inches the first year, and after that a most rapid growth takes place.

Besides the teak, there is much valuable timber in Burma, and among the most important of these is the Diospyros melanoxylon, or ebony, which grows profusely; the Lagerstrœmia, which is, after the teak, the wood most used for shipbuilding; and the Fagræ fragrans which is a most useful wood, and the Burmese themselves look upon it with great veneration; some imagining that it ought to be used solely for holy purposes.

The Dipterocarpus lævis and D. turbinatus are both curious, as they produce oil besides a very good timber. The oil is produced from the tree by making excavations at the foot, of about some seventeen to eighteen inches, after which a fire is

lighted inside the aperture, and the heat thus produced induces the oil to flow freely, and a vessel is
arranged in a convenient position to receive it. It
is possible, I am told, for a tree to produce as
much as five and thirty gallons of oil in a year.
The best charcoal is also made from this tree, so
that it appears to be a most useful specimen.

The pickled tea in Burma is a very favourite
drink, and this tea is grown both in the Northern
Shan States, and also in the Upper Chindwin.
Most of the pickled tea which is consumed by the
Burmese is grown in Yaung Baing in the Northern
Shan States. The plant yielding this tea has now
been identified as the ordinary Assam tea plant.
Two crops are secured each year; only the young
and tender leaves being taken. These, after having
been subjected to a preparation and treatment by
boiling, are sold to traders, who carry it to the
Mandalay market in long baskets, so packed that
fermentation is prevented. Mr. Bruce, the author
of the Upper Chindwin reports, states that the
gardens he saw in that region were wonderfully
healthy, considering the little care taken of them.
He thinks that tea-planting on European methods
would be a great success, if the labour difficulty
could be successfully dealt with. As with labour,
the planter need only search for red earth areas,
which are numerous all over the Upper Chindwin.
The plants become large enough to give a crop in

three years, if the garden is kept from jungle; seed is borne in eight years, and in fifteen years the trees are in full bearing, their normal existence being forty or fifty years. The profits on the trade seem to be enormous; as tea bought at the gardens at from 15 to 25 rupees for 360 lbs., is sold in Mandalay at from 60 to 140 rupees. The trader makes over cent. per cent. profit on his outlay.

CHAPTER X.

WE spent two more pleasant days at Mandalay on our return journey, one morning of which I was taken by my kind friend, Mrs. Manook, to pay a visit to a charming Burmese lady. This lady's husband had held a high position in the Customs in King Thebaw's time, and had amassed a goodly fortune. She was a most dainty person, and lived in a large brick house, and received us in a fine well-proportioned room, one corner of which was decorated by soft-hued rugs, a few chairs, and a table exquisitely laid out with every kind of lovely sweet and fruits. Pepia, water-melons, grapes, bananas, guavas, besides endless lovely little trays containing bonbons, all made, as she told us, by her own fair hands! The whole thing was served in the most delicate manner; iced water was presented to you in the most magnificent golden embossed bowls; and the soft perfume of roses and lotus flowers peeping out from a large silver vase, shed a subtle perfume through the room, and brought back lingering memories of almost forgotten fairy tales.

The lady herself was arrayed in gorgeous apparel. She was attired in a splendid pink silk tamehn, richly embroidered with silver, a white satin jacket also embroidered with large bunches of flowers, and a pale pink gossamer crêpe scarf thrown with coquettish grace over her shoulders. She wore many jewels, some of them were exceptionally fine, and the setting was not so barbaric as is generally the case with an Eastern. She had round her neck a pearl necklace and two diamond ones, and large solitaire diamonds suspended from a row of pearls. A beautiful diamond comb gleamed in her hair, besides three splendid pins, an emerald, ruby, and diamond; these were mixed in cunningly with a wreath of jasmine flowers, which contrasted excellently with her dark glossy tresses. On her arms she wore two really magnificent bangles; they were about an inch and a half in width, and they were entirely studded with enormous diamonds.

The whole scene savoured of the golden shining East, and as I sat there contemplating this really charming vision seated there between her two handmaids, who squatted near by, each fanning her with large lotus-shaped fans, which they

15

wielded with a soft-swaying movement, a dream
of Moore's " Lalla Rookh " stole over me, and
I seemed to be taking part in some delicious
mystical romance. We remained for nearly two
hours discoursing to this fascinating lady, the
conversation on my part being carried on by the
kind interpretations of my friend, Mrs. Manook.
Our fair hostess complained bitterly that her
life was so dull, as though by birth a Burmese,
her husband was a Mahometan, and she was
therefore forced to conform to the Mahometan
idea, and give up her liberty, and remain behind
the Purdah, which evidently was a very severe
trial. She said that she desired much to go back
to England with me! I ventured to suggest that
perhaps that plan would hardly find favour in her
husband's eyes. Upon which she laughed and
said that he would have to do as she wished,
otherwise the remedy was simple! She would
divorce him! An easy matter in Burma! The
two handmaids amused me immensely, as they
joined the whole time in the conversation, freely
expressing their approval or disapprobation upon
all the subjects discussed.

At parting, our courteous hostess presented me
with a photograph of herself, some exquisite
grapes, and a wonderfully precious Burmese scent;
and then with all the Eastern floweriness of language, she begged me not to forget her, and said

NATIVE VILLAGE BELOW MANDALAY.

that every day in her prayers she would pray that I might return to Mandalay.

On the 9th of March, we once more placed ourselves on board a Flotilla steamer (the *China*), and were borne down the river towards Rangoon. On the southern side of Mandalay the hills were extremely charming, and absolutely covered with

AN IRRAWADDY SAILING BOAT.

pagodas, as it is looked upon as an especially holy spot. Every tiny knoll and point was crowned by one of these tapering spires, until the whole landscape was absolutely studded with them. The country, after leaving the Mandalay hills, became very flat and uninteresting, and the little villages were not nearly as picturesque as north of Mandalay.

We tied up the first night at Pokoko, which is a very large district, and the town has a population of about 119,000, a deputy commissioner, and a certain number of native police. It does an enormous trade in boat-building, and we saw there a great number of the charming and picturesque native boats which ply the Irrawaddy. In form they rather resemble a Chinese junk, having the stern and prow both very much curved. They have a curious little house built upon them, and the steerer sits in a very elevated position in a quaint carved chair, from which he commands a splendid view of the course, and also looks most ornamental, especially when, as is often the case, he has a large Chinese umbrella arranged over his head. The sails of these boats are most picture-like; they are large square yards, and are arranged upon rings, so that they pull backwards and forwards like curtains! These boats can, of course, only go before the wind, a flock of them speeding up or down the river look perfectly lovely, like pure white birds.

About an hour after leaving Pokoko, we passed by the great and wonderful Pagahn.

Pagahn is the Benares or Holy City of Burma, but no Holy City in the world can boast of such a multiplicity of shrines and temples as this city can. It is now unfortunately quite deserted, and the jungle is fast growing over the mass of glorious

PAGAHN.

architecture which it contains. Greedy tendrils
and dank grasses are creeping and crawling over
these wondrous shrines, and laying green damp
fingers upon the rich carving and ornamentation,
and here and there pushing their heads through
the clefts which time has made.

The form of these shrines is quite dissimilar to
those in other parts of Burma. Colonel Yule, in
his mission to Ava, says that in Pagahn there are
found every form of temple. The bell-shaped
pyramid of dead brickwork; the square or octa-
gonal cell, containing an image of Buddha; the
bluff, knob-like dome of the Ceylon dagobats; and
the fantastic bo-payah or pumpkin pagoda; but,
most curiously, the form which predominates is
that of the cruciform vaulted temple.

Pagahn was the capital until 1284 A.D., when the
Chinese sent a huge army there to avenge the
murder of their ambassador, and the then King of
Burma is said to have demolished six thousand
temples to strengthen the fortifications; but a
prophecy, which was said to have been discovered
under the ruins of one of these desecrated shrines,
terrified him so greatly that he decamped quickly
in a southern direction, abandoning the city which
has ever since that time been utterly deserted.
The temples, even in their ruined condition, are
some of the most interesting remains to be found
anywhere, and present a marvellous picture.

Their decoration, carving, and design are quite
unexampled, and can well vie with those of
India. There are said to be 9,999 shrines, but
I should imagine that this was possibly a slight
exaggeration! The view of Pagahn from the
river, though not at all distinct, is curious; the
endless spires, domes, and minarets appearing in
the far distance and lying against the horizon like
a pale blue grey mist, while along the banks of
the river, for the space of eight miles, and two
miles in width, stray a multitude of pagodas of
every shape and size, and in every possible condition; they present a most strange sight, the
ground simply bristles with them.

After leaving Pagahn the country improved, and
a low range of mountains rose gradually up close
to the river. The next place of interest that we
stopped at was Zeymangyaung, which is close to
some large oil wells, from which there is now
a large export. Burma is assuredly a favoured
land, and her soil is rich in treasures of varied
quality. She has silver, copper, jewels, gold, and
oil; verily a list culled from " The Arabian
Nights," though, of course, at present many of the
minerals have not been worked. The villages, as
we proceeded further south, became again more
picturesque, and were once more set in their delightful green frames of palms, mango, and peepul.

We tied up the second night at Mimbu, which

PAGAHN.

is also a place of some importance ; and the following morning, the 11th of March, we reached Minhla, which is interesting, as it was the old boundary line between Upper and Lower Burma. The country between that and Prome is charming, not beautiful in the grand, glorious way that the defiles are farther north, but with a *riante*, joyous luxuriance and colour which makes it very attractive. As you approach to within fifteen miles of Prome, the hills stray down quite close to the river banks, and you pass through what might almost be called a defile ; in parts, the river widens out into a huge lake surrounded by hills which are clothed with a dense mass of bamboo, which wave and shimmer in the sunlight, and bend their graceful heads to the kisses of each soft breeze.

Prome itself possesses a most captivating situation. It stands rather high with the mighty Irrawaddy flowing silently at its feet, while across, on the opposite shore, it looks upon a glorious range of hills whose delicate wistful outlines are drawn out in the softest of lights and shades. Prome is quite a large place, and possesses a Dak bungalow of very comfortable proportions. It is essentially an attractive place. The native houses are particularly picturesque and set in most luxuriant frames of bananas and waving palms. The pagoda at Prome is quite one of the most

beautiful in Burma. It is a golden one, but not
nearly so large as the Shway Dagohn at Rangoon,
but for its size it is quite as lovely. It stands like
its Rangoon brother on a hill and overlooks with a
benign glance the town beneath. It is approached
on four sides by long flights of steps which are
enclosed by beautiful carved roofs, and these give
upon a large paved space, in the centre of which
rises the lovely gilded tapering shrine surrounded
by a fascinating company of tiny golden disciples,
which look like a miniature army stationed there to
protect their king. Round the paved space and
flanking the graceful glittering company are four
portals which lead to the steep flights of steps.
Each of these entrances has an exquisitely carved
canopy composed of endless airy roofs tapering
away and away until they finish in a delicate spire.
Between these gates were several shrines enclosing images of Buddha, and fair groups of white
pagodas mingled with these shrines and formed a
wall of temples round the outer space.

The whole was intensely captivating, and struck
one as possessed of a singular grace and charm
especially when seen as we saw it in the soft sunlight glow which decked the golden company with
crowns of radiance, while the tenderest of breezes
shook the tiny tinkling bells on each golden Htee
and caused them to ring a sweet melodious cadence.
The date of this lovely shrine, the Shwe San-Daw

PROME.

as it is called, is said to be 441 B.C., a hundred and thirty years after the birth of Buddha, its age thus being 2,336 years.

Shortly after leaving Prome, there stretches along the banks of the river for some considerable space a wonderful company of carved Buddhas. These extraordinary and grotesque images are carved out of the solid rock, and are really of very great interest from the ingenuity with which this has been effected. After leaving the Buddhas, the river has little to offer in the way of beauty; the country that you pass through is flat, and mostly under rice cultivation, and therefore lacks picturesqueness, and there is nothing of remarkable interest until you once more reach Rangoon.

I have said that the Burmese are extremely superstitious, but I have not given any account of their superstitions, which I do not think that anything can exaggerate. Their fear and dread of evil spirits and their strong belief in charms is most extraordinary. They carry and have tattooed upon them all kinds of curious things as preventions against drowning or any other death or evil; they sometimes insert coins under the skin. We saw two men in the prison at Mandalay (Dacoits I believe they were) with many quite large pieces of money imbedded in their flesh, and these coins were supposed to protect them from all sorts of misfortune, but, unluckily for them, they had not

16

alas! prevented their being caught and put in prison! One of the most curious things regarding this belief is that when the efficacy of these charms is proved to be absolutely worthless, a ready excuse is always forthcoming. Something was wanting when they procured the charm, or it was not a lucky moment, or they wore it in a wrong manner; in fact, any apology is made for them rather than disbelieve that they are useless.

The especial fear which the Burmese suffer from more than anything else is their dread of nats (spirits) and demons. The belief in these extremely annoying personages torments and troubles their minds to an amazing degree, and everything is done to propitiate these evil spirits. Shrines are erected outside a village for the especial nat who is supposed to inhabit that neighbourhood. These shrines vary very much in size and design. Sometimes they consist only of a bamboo cage hung from a tree in which is placed a small image. There is generally an aperture in the cage to allow the extra superstitious person to put in offerings of food or water for the nat. In other places the shrines are on far more elaborate lines. Should the village be large the shrine is much more pretentious, in some places taking the form of quite a large temple with an effigy of the nat inside it.

They have one of the most curious, not to say

disagreeable, specifics against cholera. Should it
be your misfortune to be in a Burman village when
that dread malady is hovering near, you might
imagine that the whole population had suddenly,
without any warning, become hopeless raving
lunatics. They rush upon the roofs of their
houses and shriek and yell and scream, accom-
panying this fearful din by beating upon any vessel,
gong, drum, pot, or kettle that they can lay hands
upon until the whole air is filled with a deafening,
vibrating wave of sound which rises up on all sides
with fiendish intensity. Each strives to outdo his
neighbour until the howls and shrieks of the popu-
lace are like a thousand devils from Dante's Inferno
let loose upon the earth. This waste of valuable
tissue is undertaken in the vain and illusive belief
that if there is sufficient noise it will scare away
the evil spirits or nats who it is supposed bring the
cholera.

The worship of nats and spirits is much depre-
cated by the Buddhist religion, but notwithstanding
this, it still has an enormous hold upon the people's
very superstitious minds.

The word "nat" is a very difficult one to fully
explain. The Burmese imagine that there are two
species of these spirits; one are people who live in
what is termed the six lower heavens, called also
dewahs, whose king, it is supposed, visits the earth
at the new year, while the others are spirits of

the water, air, and forest, in fact, fairies, pixies,
brownies, things, which as children we all believed
in, that is if we were well-brought-up children!
Probably the new *fin de siècle* child has not so
much belief left in him as to look on a fairy ring
with awe, or to gaze out on a moonlight night and
see the elves hiding under the red toad-stools ; he
would laugh at such old-world notions and bring
down some scientific reasoning to prove its impos-
sibility : but we old-fashioned children, like the
Burmese, still cling to our old faiths, and like to
believe in the good and bad fairies, though with
the Burmese, and even more so with other tribes,
such as the Kachins, these nats appear to be all
more or less bad and malevolent people, who need
a great deal of coaxing and propitiating, and gifts
of all kinds are offered to induce these spirits to
leave mortals in peace. The Kachins often erect
outside their villages all sorts of curious things
as protection against the nats, such as spears, bows
and arrows, and anything that may form an im-
pediment to the nats.

The household nat rejoices in the name of Min-
mahgayee, and he is a kind of guardian to the
house, and the very devout nat worshippers will
actually take the trouble of covering certain posts
of the house with a cotton cloth, as it is supposed
that he dwells upon these posts, and I conclude in
some occult way has signified his especial predilec-

tion for white cloth! I believe that the household nat is not what we should term a good brownie, who inhabits the house with the wish to bring the inhabitants happiness and good fortune ; on the contrary, he is a selfish, short-tempered sort of person, who simply takes up his abode there because it happens to suit his convenience, and if not kept in a good humour he might bring dire trouble upon his entertainers. But it is believed that should robbers or evil-minded people come and attack the house he would strike them with some foul complaint, not the least as a kindly action to his host, but merely to preserve the house for himself, as it would be tiresome for him to move ; thus, in his own egotistical way, he is useful to the householder.

Beside the nat of the house there is another especial nat for the village, and he appears to be quite as tiresome and exigent a person, and expects quite as much attention and gifts as the other, and it is for his pleasure that the shrines are erected outside the villages.

The very low class Talaings, who are most superstitious, will often before partaking of food breathe a prayer to the nat of the village. A 'ewer of water is also nearly always to be found in a Burman house, this is also in some way a protection against nats.

In some of the really remote villages in the

jungle there is practised by the Talaings a most
weird and curious function which is performed
should one of the community fall sick, or any
illness threaten the community. An enormous
feast is prepared of the usual staple foods, rice,
currie, chickens, &c. These dainties are collected
together at a place outside the village, and are
generally placed upon some kind of raised structure. Every one in the village has to take a part
in this function. Many of them personating nats,
witches, or beeloos, while others pretend to be dogs
and other animals, putting themselves upon their
hands and knees and crawling about. When these
people are supposed to have become sufficiently
possessed with spirits, the rest of the village sally
out and inquire of them whether the sick will
recover. The answer is, of course, always in the
affirmative, after which the people precipitate
themselves into the forest, and armed with a piece
of canvas or cloth, which they cast over any low
brushwood or mound of grass, endeavour to en-
trap butterflies very much in the way schoolboys
go after these insects. They then carefully squeeze
up the handkerchief with the precious animal inside and return to the infected village where they
open the handkerchief and shake it out over the
sufferers. They are supposed to have caught what
is termed the "lehp-bya," a kind of spirit which has
some occult connection with the sick man, and

whose absence, it is supposed, has produced the illness. When the butterfly returns to its own and proper dwelling-place the scourge will be removed. This function is very little in fashion now, and will probably soon entirely disappear.

In some parts of Burma they still have nat feasts. A kind of effigy of a nat being constructed, which is paraded round the rice fields and then has gifts offered to it. There are, I am told, some more important nats, who appear to be peculiarly malignant. There is one called Moung Inn Gyee, who is supposed to inhabit the water and cause death to any who may be unlucky enough to fall into his presence. He has, I believe, an especial festival to himself to try and induce him to abstain from his evil ways!

There is another of these charming individuals who rejoices in the name of Moung Min Gyee, who is inclined to be a little too fond of spirituous liquors, and has to have rice spirit presented to him. One would suggest a blue ribbon being more efficacious!

When a Burman departs upon a journey he has a habit of placing (if superstitious) a bunch of bananas on the pole of his cart or on the prow of his boat, which is intended as a conciliatory offering to the particular nat spirit of the country he purposes to pass through. When a boat race is going to take place it is often the custom for both crews to row over the course previous to the race with offerings for the nat spirit of the river. One of the theories concerning nats is that persons who have been executed or meet with a violent death become nats and demons, and haunt the spot where they were killed; another idea about them is that they were the spirits of monks and nuns whose lives had not been as saintly and pure as they might have been, and that after death they became evil spirits.

The Burman's measurement of time is very quaint. Should you inquire how long it would take to perform a certain thing, he replies, "As long as it takes to chew three betel nuts, or as long as two pots of rice take to boil ; or it happened at the hour when the young men go a-courting, or when the monks go a-begging, or before the sky was bright." They have a very fantastic mode of expression, and are often unconsciously very poetical in some of their ideas; for instance, their name for hail is the "rain flower." The Burman's belief in omens is very strong. In the month when Venus is invisible, or in the month when there is an earthquake or an eclipse happens on the first or last day of the month, it is believed to be unlucky to cut your hair, marry, or to build a pagoda !

CHAPTER XI.

THE rice fields cover such an enormous tract of land in Burma, and the paddy is such a valuable and important product of the country, that I think a few words upon its cultivation would not come amiss in this little work. There are roughly, I believe, about two and a half millions of acres given up to the cultivation of this valuable grain. The best quality of rice comes from the low-lying lands near to the Irrawaddy, where the ground is swampy; and flooded every year by the rising of the river.

In other parts of the country where the land is drier and more elevated, irrigation has to be resorted to, and on the hillsides, where the moisture runs off with great rapidity, the cultivation is a work of some difficulty and requires a good deal of labour.

A rice farm on a soft, wet soil is the easiest and laziest form of farming imaginable, and one which therefore greatly commends itself to a Burman ; though it is only fair to him to say that it is the thing that he does extremely well.

Early in June, when the south-west monsoon begins and the rain descends in pailfuls, the ground is soon brought into a pleasing and satisfactory state of soft, pulpy mud. When this happy state of things has been achieved, the Burman begins to plough, which he does with oxen or with the water buffalo. The farmer either drives the team himself or, should this prove too irksome a task, he makes use of his family in this particular. Farms in Burma are not of large extent, being usually between ten to twenty acres, so that the ploughing is not a long process and is soon completed. It is the custom to have nurseries on the higher ground, where the rice seed is prepared for the lower lands. A month or two has to elapse before the operation of planting can be undertaken, so that the Burman has a pleasant time of repose and ease between his ploughing and planting, which suits him admirably. At the beginning of August the land which has been thus prepared in the lower country has become less saturated with moisture, and it is therefore ready to receive the plants from the nursery, which have by this time attained a fair size. These are then transplanted and placed in the wet ground at intervals of a few inches. This work is also generally performed by

the women and children, while the farmer not
unfrequently looks calmly on enjoying his ease
with of course the much-beloved cheroot! After
this latter process has been completed there is
nothing remaining but to await what Providence
sends in the way of a good harvest. This waiting
a Burman rather enjoys, the delightful peace of
knowing there is nothing further to be done;
nothing left to do but to contemplate the ripen-
ing paddy, and dream of the rupees that it is
going to bring, and how these rupees will be
spent, makes food for many a delightful surmise.
Should the dire misfortune occur of an excessive
rainfall after the planting, which should rot
the roots, all has to be done over again, which
must be a great trial of patience, but a Burman takes everything easily and pleasantly, and
probably only laughs.

In November the harvest takes place, and the
labour for this is generally imported from Upper
Burma. The paddy is never in Burma, as is the
case in Europe, cut close to the ground, the ears
being the only portion taken, and the straw is then
burnt in the fields and produces a slight manure.
This burning is done in March and April, and on
our way to Mandalay we saw many of these curious
little fires running up and down the hillsides or
in other places traversing the flat ground. They
looked most picturesque those little rivers of

flames, which shot up and flickered in the gloaming like a true will-o'-the-wisp.

The harvest is not of long duration, and the cutting is soon accomplished. The manner of treating the rice after the cutting is still most primitive, as it is trodden out by oxen. When the husk has thus been removed, the grain is winnowed. There are now a few hand winnowing machines in use, but more often the rice is winnowed by the very simple process of being emptied down a slight inclined plane constructed of a bamboo mat. The paddy slips down this and then falls to the ground, the lighter parts and such pieces of straw and husk being carried away by the wind. One can hardly imagine that the result would be very complete or satisfactory, but it is the easiest way of accomplishing it, and therefore of course presents an attraction to a Burman. After this last process the rice is considered ready for sale, and there is nothing left to be done except to load the rice boat and go down the creek to Rangoon.

The cultivation of rice would have been, one would imagine, a most profitable one to the farmer, as I am told his rent per acre is something like three shillings; and the usual amount of paddy per acre is from seventy to one hundred bushels, while in less luxuriant land about half the quantity is secured. At Rangoon the price of rice per maund,

or eighty pounds, is about four to five shillings.
Thus one would imagine that a Burmese farmer
would have an infinitely better time than an
English one, and ought certainly to grow rich;
and so he probably would if it were not for his
pleasure-loving character and his intense dislike
to thrift and saving, and still more to his delight
in gambling.

This gambling leads to debt, and debt leads
to borrowing, and borrowing, alas! tempts those
altogether despicable characters of Madras moneylenders. These people prey upon the easy-going
Burman, and convert themselves into what might
almost be termed "middlemen." In almost
every village one of these rascals takes up his
abode, and when the too reckless Burman is in
want of money, the tempter is ready at his
elbow offering to lend what is required. But the
reckoning day, alas! comes swiftly, and the Madras
chetty exacts the very last "pound of flesh," or, in
other words, a percentage which is absolutely
abominable and preposterous, varying from 8 to
12 per cent. a month, which can only be paid
by the never-failing paddy; therefore it is to
the chetty's interest that the price of rice should
be kept up, and it is greatly due to their inter-
ference that so many scandalous practices with
regard to the weight of the paddy have been in
use.   In old days, before the great competition

existed, the price remained about the same; but now with the enormous increase of mills the bidding between farmers has naturally become great, and the ruses resorted to by the Burmese, or the moneylenders, to get as much as they can and to make the weight of the baskets as great as possible are many and full of resource.

A certain size of basket was at length determined upon by all the firms, but even this laudable effort was of no avail, as it was tampered with and all kinds of things were used, and even, in some cases, false bottoms were inserted.

I have said that in the low, wet-lying country the cultivation of rice was an easy task, but this cannot be said of the "toung-ya" or where the hills have been cleared. This needs a very laborious effort to make the ground possible, as the clearing and felling of thick forests and undergrowth means an infinity of work.

The soil, too, on the higher hill ground, is not, as in the plains, rich, fertile, and independent of manure, and it is therefore necessary before planting the rice to burn the timber that has been felled and the undergrowth, and then to dig the ashes well into the soil so as to produce a kind of manure.

The clearing of these dense jungle forests is a lengthy and difficult work; but the Burmese are not without resource and ingenuity in this as in

many other ways, and on the steep hillsides the really brilliant idea struck them of letting the upper part of the forests knock down the lower trees as they fell. They therefore cut only a notch in the lowest trees, which notch they increased in size as they mounted up the hill, till with the highest trees they carried the notch entirely through the tree, and in its fall it carried with it the lower ones till the forest fell down like a set of ninepins, each falling tree crashing into another in rotation until they reached the bottom and the whole thing was levelled to the ground.

This land is only very rudely prepared, and it is the custom to mix cotton seed with the rice—the latter is not at all of the same quality as that grown upon the plains and is not used for export, but merely as a food for the hill tribes, who cultivate it. The soil in these hill clearings is not sufficiently fertile to grow rice for many years following, consequently a new clearing has to be made nearly every year, and this is certainly by no means an economical or commendable process, and is looked upon with great disfavour by the forest officers.

The busy time at the rice mills is from January to May, when the river is crowded with ships of every condition, large, small, good, bad, and indifferent—all come to take away the rice, and it presents a very gay and animated scene. The

picturesque rice boats are jostling each other in
the creeks, and their owners are indulging in a
good deal of well-meant chaff. It is not difficult to
estimate the amount of rice which each boat bears,
as it is generally concluded that about 100 lbs.
goes to a rower, therefore a boat with three rowers
has about 300 lbs.; six rowers, 600 lbs.; seven
rowers, 700 lbs., and so on. There are crowds of
coolies clambering up and down the banks between
the boats and the godowns, and even the Burmese
show a certain amount of excitement and energy,
and deign to give a little help in the unloading of
the rice. The water all round the rice boats and
near to the shore is thick with paddy husk, which
does not enhance the beauty or cleanness of the
river. It has been tried to turn this into fuel,
but up to the present time the efforts made have
unfortunately not been successful.

The screaming and shrieking that go on help,
I conclude, considerably in the sale of the paddy,
otherwise the waste of time must be great. In
any case the throats of the brokers who rush about
in their little dugouts making the bargains for
their firms must suffer materially, and one would
think that they must become hoarse for the rest of
the year! The excitement is enormous, and all
sorts of queer cabalistic signs pass between these
gentlemen when they meet each other.

If outside is noise, heat, and glare, inside the

godowns and mills can hardly be said to be an improvement. There the dust gets into your eyes and mouth and parches your throat, and the noise thunders round you and threatens to leave you permanently deaf for life, while the air seems ladened with thousands of particles which stifle you. The only thing which can be looked upon as a trifle better inside is the absence of glare. The semi-darkness is an immense relief after the scorching light without.

At the first moment that you enter you see nothing, and then gradually you behold shadowy, ghostly figures rising out of the darkness, working at great mounds of rice which are waiting to be measured, while rows of coolies ladened with baskets amble backwards and forwards. Here, also, shrieking and screaming seems the order of the day, and that, mixed with the constant "rush" of the pouring paddy, makes a din and pandemonium worthy of the betting ring on any large race-course. Paddy seems to surround and engulf you. All the rice puddings of your youth seem suddenly to have risen up from the dead past like some horrible nightmare and be mocking at you, and you wonder vaguely if you will ever wish to behold that homely dish again. On one side is a real mountain of rice up which coolies follow each other and empty basket upon basket. Lower down more coolies are filling bins with the grain from this same mountain. Through these bins the rice passes into double sieves, which sieves are kept continually in motion by machinery and the grain is thus cleansed from all pieces of straw, earth, or foreign matter which has got among it. After the sieve process it still has to pass through two or three other processes. When the grain falls through the sieves, it is deftly caught in a series of little buckets which are attached to a leather band, and in these vessels is conveyed to the top floor of the mill. From thence it descends to the stores and is then handed over to the fans, which separate it entirely from the husk.

After the fans it is sent down to the weighing floor, and from thence it is again conveyed to what is termed the sewing floors, where rows of charming little Burmese maidens are seated, sewing up the bags of rice, their neat little fingers going in and out with great rapidity and precision. The sewing department evidently requires much supervision! and gets occasionally more than its fair share, especially from a young and susceptible godown wallah. One can hardly wonder or blame him, as one's eyes wanders over the neat little row of figures who, in spite of their work, laugh and chatter together, and find time to cast many roguish glances at those around.

A rice mill is very like a flour mill in the matter of white dust that creeps over everything, and the

coolies present a most quaint appearance with
their whitened hair and eyebrows and black,
shining faces.   One is thankful to emerge again
from the roaring noise of the mill machinery, even
though one has to brave that scorching, glaring
sunshine which burns and frizzles one in such a
manner that one is almost led to wonder if by
some inadvertency the kitchen fire has wandered
up into the sky and is calmly sitting over one's
head.   The rice is now being conveyed over to
another godown, there to await trans-shipment and
be sent away to all parts of the world.   One
is quite thankful when one gets so far, to see the
great bags disappearing on the necks of the lank
Chittagonian backs.   One's head feels dizzy with
the noise of the shrieking, and the machinery
seems to be still grinding into your brain, and you
are almost inclined to feel that no rice pudding,
not even one belonging to your happiest nursery
days, was ever worth such a morning.

CHAPTER XII

POHN-GYEES.

I HAVE said that the pagodas in Burma are
almost as difficult to number as the sands of
the sea! I should also say that the Pohn-gyee
koungs would be nearly as hard to count. In
Thebaw's time there were hundreds of these religious houses which were supported entirely by the
Crown, as it was believed to be a great act of merit
to erect and maintain one of these monasteries.
Since our occupation the koungs have had to look
for their maintenance to the pious population to
clothe and feed the monks, though I believe that
the Government does give a certain grant to a
Pohn-gyee school if they will undertake to teach
really useful knowledge. The sole education that
the people received previous to our annexation
came, of course, through the monastic schools.
Every Burman must become a Pohn-gyee for at
least one day of his life " if he would be other than
a brute beast," but they generally remain in the

monastery for one Lent, which means about four
months, or sometimes, if very pious, for two Lents.
A Pohn-gyee can take his vows for any length of
time that he wills, and should he desire at any

POHN-GYEES TEACHING.

time to cast them off and go forth again into the
world, it is permitted that he should do so.

No doubt Buddha was a real diplomatist, for in-
sisting upon this law of conscription, as it might

be called, or of obliging every layman to take upon
him for a certain period the vows and duties of
a priest; he thus imperceptibly gained a thorough
religious hold upon all classes of the nation; and
religion filtered through the whole community far
more widely and easily, as each person felt that he,
individually, was a part of the great whole. The
line which in so many countries is so sternly drawn
between priest and layman does not in Burma exist
to the same severe extent, and undoubtedly this
tends to make a more religious population.

The monasteries, I have already said, are supported entirely by the voluntary contributions of
the inhabitants. Each morning, at a certain hour,
you see large companies of Pohn-gyees parading
the streets, each with a large brass begging-pot
suspended round his neck. These pots resemble
a soup-tureen with a flat lid, and into these vessels
are put the offerings of food made by the faithful.
The monk stands before each door, and in a
few minutes you see the women issue out and
drop into it rice, or bananas, or curry, and the
Pohn-gyee then passes silently on his way. He
returns no thanks to the giver by word or gesture,
as it is supposed that the favour is hers who
bestows and is thus allowed to perform such an act
of merit as feeding a Pohn-gyee! It is a most
picturesque sight to watch the long stream of
begging monks issuing out on their rounds.

They are arrayed in soft-coloured yellow robes which are supposed to resemble the shrouds of the dead, and are dyed to the especial tint to imitate earth stains. They nearly always carry a lotus-shaped fan made of a palm leaf, with which they are supposed to shade their eyes from lighting upon any fair maidens! Whether they are always very rigorous in their use of these is, I think, a little doubtful, though, certainly, against the blandishments of the little Burmese girls they are a most necessary precaution!

Besides the begging-pot and fan, they have a "kaban" or leathern girdle, a "pe-koht," a short-handled axe for cutting firewood, an "att," a needle, and a "yaysit," a strainer for filtering water, so that there may be no chance of their unknowingly taking human life by imbibing microbes!

The ceremony of making a boy a Pohn-gyee (or Buddhist baptism as it might be called) is most curious, and we were fortunate enough to witness one of these functions at Mandalay. The boy was about the age of twelve years; he was arrayed in his most gorgeous apparel and decked with all the family jewels. He was then mounted upon a pony (sometimes they are placed upon a gaily decorated car) and paraded round the town, shaded by a gold umbrella. He stopped at the houses of his relations to offer them a greeting

and bid them farewell. The relations, in return
for the visit, bestowed gifts and sometimes money
to aid with the expense of the ceremony. A
band of music preceded the boy, and many of
his friends and relations attended him in procession, the girls dancing and the men singing.
At the parents' house, or, as I witnessed it, in
a temporary building, great preparations had been
made. The room was decorated with huge mirrors
and plants. A high daïs was erected at one end,
on which sat the head of the koung to which the
boy was to be admitted, around him were grouped
many Pohn-gyees, and in front of them were
placed endless offerings, which had been presented, such as fruit, rice, mats, and yellow cloth
for the monks' robes. The younger monks were
seated in a long line, and were counselled to carefully shade their faces with their large lotus-shaped
fans, so that their eyes might not rest upon the
bewitching crowd of charming dark-eyed damsels
who were sitting near, laughing and joking together
with intense merriment, their hair decked with
flowers, and their soft pink tamehns hanging in
graceful folds.

The boy proceeded to divest himself of his gay
clothes, and donned a piece of white cloth which
he bound round his loins. His head was then
shaved, his hair being appropriated by his mother,
who used it to increase the size of her own chignon!

After the shaving the boy's head was washed with a decoction made from the seeds and bark of Kin-bo-hn-thee, and rubbed with saffron. He then bathed, and once more arrayed himself in his gorgeous apparel and presented himself to the head of the koung, prostrating himself three times, and begged for admission to the Holy Assembly as a neophyte. The superior of the monastery then bestowed upon him the yellow robe, begging pot, &c., and he was duly equipped and took his place among the novices.

A band performed loudly all the time, the musicians being enclosed in a curious little round barricade. The instruments consisted of a Soung (harp), Patayah (cymbal), constructed of bamboo and played with small trumpets, Palway (flute), See (a small cymbal), and Hnè, which resembles bag-pipes, and makes nearly as much noise. After the actual ceremony had been performed, of course amusement must needs step in and have a finger in the pie. Feasting and a Pwè followed, the latter I can testify to having lasted with short cessations for twenty-four hours! As this ceremony took place within a few yards of where I was staying, my ears and my nerves impressed the fact disagreeably upon my mind.

Pohn-gyees are fond of ceremonies, and no doubt they show a certain wisdom in fostering the love of a pageant, which every nation loves in its

heart, particularly an Eastern one, and to a Burman
these shows impress his religion upon his mind.
The greatest ceremony of all is enacted when a
Pohn-gyee dies, particularly should he be a much

A BEGGING MONK.

venerated one. In life they lead a tranquil, easy
existence, the even tenour is not often ruffled.
They are spared the weary anxiety for the morrow,
as they are fed and clothed by the pious population,

and their duties can hardly be described as arduous,
as they only consist in giving instruction to a few
boys. They begin their day early, and intone a
short morning service, after which a few menial
duties have to be performed, and then a meditation
upon the missions of life—meditation being peculiarly meritorious. A light repast follows upon
that, and then a certain time is set apart for
study, after which the begging hour has arrived,
and they issue out in a long line and wend their
way to the village. Whether they really sustain
life solely upon the heterogeneous food which is
bestowed upon them is I believe now rather doubtful, as things have become more lax, and there are
rumours that a more dainty repast is cooked for
them at the koung, while the pious offerings are
bestowed upon the scholars, a certain portion being
always reserved for presentation to Buddha. They
pass the rest of the day in conversation, more
meditation, in teaching reading, and in a staid
constitutional.

Another and very beautiful little service is performed at about eight o'clock, and vespers are
intoned before an image of Buddha, after which
one of the novices cries out in a clear voice the
hour, the day, the week, the day of the month, and
the number of the year.

No Pohn-gyee is permitted to partake of food
after mid-day, nor is he allowed to be without the

monastery after sunset. Excommunication is, I believe, occasionally practised, and the service of unfrocking a Pohn-gyee is a very impressive one. The monks surround the culprit, and a portion of the Kammamah, that which is usually read to drive sickness and evil spirits away, is recited. His yellow robe is then taken from off him, and his begging pot is reversed, and he is thrust out of the monastery. He is in a terribly bad plight, as no one may speak to him; he can neither buy nor sell, nor is it even permitted for him to drink from one of the jars which stand near to the rest-houses; in fact his position is as much of an outcast as a pagoda slave. It has been occasionally the practice of these koungs, where the district has been particularly notorious for its evil doings, to punish the inhabitants by refusing to go begging, and so withholding from them the great merit which falls upon those who feed a Pohn-gyee. This measure has generally had a most salutary effect, the most abandoned being brought to see the evil of their ways.

A Pohn-gyee receives all through his life immense reverence and respect, but when death claims him, this respect and veneration bursts out and displays itself by the most gorgeous ceremony which is then performed. A Pohn-gyee, it is believed, does not die like a layman, or even a king. The Pohn-gyee's spirit rises to the highest heaven of nats, or to the meditative state of Zahn. Every Pohn-gyee is burnt with a certain ceremony; but a Pohn-gyee who is celebrated for his ascetic life, his many Lents and great merit, is burnt with marvellous rites, and what is termed a Pohn-gyee Byan.

When death has claimed the holy man, the body is washed by his chief supporters. The intestines are removed and buried in the monastery grounds or near to a pagoda, and the body is then embalmed and occasionally a layer of wax is spread over it, but generally it is simply swathed in a white linen shroud and the whole is varnished with wood oil, in order that should it be desired the corpse may be entirely covered in gold leaf, which is always effected unless the neighbourhood should be very poor, in which case the yellow robes are substituted. The body is then encased in two coffins, the inner one being the hollowed-out trunk of a tree, and this occasionally is found rather hard to fit the departed Pohn-gyee into; and there have been little difficulties about inducing the lid to close, but this is of rare occurrence, as the holy men are usually of very meagre proportions. The outer coffin, or Payoung Bohng, as it is called, is as magnificent as it is possible for them to make, and as the money (which is subscribed) will permit. It is of course richly gilded and covered with tinsel and inlay of looking-glass.

The great object after this is to collect as much money as they can, so as to make the last rites as full of splendour as it is possible. The corpse meanwhile is deposited in a temporary edifice. The excellency of this structure depends upon the degree of holiness attained by the departed. It is usually constructed of teak wood, open all round, surmounted with the airy ecclesiastical roofs supported by pillars. The coffin is placed within this edifice upon a raised daïs, and it has a white umbrella suspended above it. The body remains lying in state for several months, it may be even for a year, and during this time funds are being collected for the great final ceremony. Throughout the time of the lying-in-state many festivals are celebrated, and pilgrims come from great distances to visit the corpse, and bring offerings of fruits and flowers, and contribute their little all to the great Pohn-gyee Byan, which ceremony never takes place in Lent.

At length when sufficient money has been collected, a space in near proximity to the town is cleared of the jungle, and a funeral pyre is erected. It is usually constructed of bamboo with bright-coloured paper, matting, pasteboard brilliantly painted, and the dearly loved tinsel. It takes the form of a spire widened out at the base, and with seven airy roofs tapering away. These seven roofs are supposed by some to imply

figuratively the number of heavens of the nat-
dewahs. The entire height of the pyre is sometimes enormous, measuring to the top of the
spire some forty or fifty feet, but it is upon a

THE PYRE.

platform about twenty feet from the ground that
the body of the Pohn-gyee is placed. The next
thing to discover is a lucky day; and when that
has been found, the great ceremony is announced

to take place, and hundreds of people flock from far and near. When all is in readiness the corpse is placed with great ceremony upon a strong and curiously built four-wheeled car, which is of course surmounted by a canopy of the same spire-like form, and then takes place the most extraordinary, and to us the most unseemly, performance. Two or occasionally four strong ropes are attached to the car, and the most able-bodied and muscular of the men engage in an uproarious tug of war; some striving to draw the car in one direction, the others frantically opposing their efforts. The excitement during the proceedings knows no bounds, and becomes more intense as the battle continues. The air is rent with the shouts of the victors or with the groans of the vanquished. No especial sides are decided upon, but there are always plenty of willing applicants to aid the losing party. The contest lasts often for four or five hours, and sometimes longer. Mr. Scott affirms as the reason for this curious and to us very irreverent spectacle that it is looked upon as an immense act of merit to drag a Pohn-gyee's body to the pyre, and it is believed that the Koothoh, or merit, falls upon all who have been victorious in the tug of war. At length, after the corpse has passed through all these vicissitudes, it is at last deposited upon the pyre, and is surrounded by a quantity of combustible material which is stacked all round. And now

nothing remains but the lighting, which one would,
in one's ignorance, have imagined to be no very
difficult matter. But it is unwise ever to prog-
nosticate the manner that a Burman will do anything, and in this instance his idea is original
to say the least of it. The pyre is lighted by
rockets and guns fired from a distance of about

A POHN-GYEE PYAN.

forty or fifty yards. The rockets have been in
preparation for many weeks before, and have been
paraded round the town in procession by the
persons who have manufactured them. The guns
are of a most primitive form, and are constructed
out of the stems of trees hollowed out and filled
with combustibles. Some of them are enormous,
measuring eight or nine feet long and four or

five feet in circumference. The largest of them
are mounted upon carts, while others are guided
to the pyre by ropes, along which the rocket
slides by means of a kind of twisted cane. When
the vital moment arrives and the longed-for
signal is given, the rockets do their best to go off.
Some succeed, others only fizz up and do nothing,
except probably injure some of the audience, while
others refuse to do anything. At last one lucky
shot goes right into the centre of the pyre and the
flames suddenly spurt out and fly upwards, their
red tongues curling round the airy roofs which
descend one by one, until the last little part of
the flimsy fabric remains for an instant poised as
it were in mid-air, and then that falls and the
whole becomes a burning blazing mass. As the
last roof tumbles the popular excitement knows
no bounds. They shout and scream, and dance
and tear their clothes and hair, and behave like
a grotesque company of lunatics.

When the embers have cooled, the Pohn-gyees
search for any bones that may be left, and these
are carefully interred near to a pagoda. If the
man should have been very saintly, they are
occasionally pounded down and made into paste
with thitsee, and then moulded into an image
of Buddha, which is presented to the monastery.

CHAPTER XIII.

CONCERNING the language of Burma a great deal that is interesting might be written. To listen to it has a soft guttural sound, and might be compared not unbecomingly to Spanish. It is a most difficult language for an Englishman to thoroughly master, on account of it being a very poor language in richness or profusion of expression, and thus the same word, uttered with a very slight difference of accent, stands for many different things. For instance, the word "koung" signifies monastery in one instance, and cat in another, if pronounced with a slightly different accent. The difference of pronunciation is so very minute and infinitesimal that to a foreigner it is almost imperceptible, and this makes Burmese a language which is a terrible trial of patience, especially to English people, who do not as a rule, catch quickly the shades of intonation as they speak more by visual demonstration than by oral sound. No doubt to an

Italian or to a Spaniard this would prove a far less difficulty to be overcome, as their sense of sound is so infinitely quicker and more acute. The Burmese language is monosyllabic, and has not as in the case of so many other languages abandoned its one syllable and joined the two together. The Burmese have preserved their language intact in that particular. Its alphabet, which is called Thembon-gyee, or great basket of learning, is derived from the ancient Magadhi, but the characters are entirely Burmese.

The alphabet is a most voluminous work in itself, as it contains ten vowels, thirty-two consonants, vowel consonants to the number of 10 × 32, besides many characters which express combinations of letters. Burmese, like all Eastern languages, partakes largely of the florid floweriness of the East, and possesses many expressions of honour and respect. *Daw* is a favourite form to be placed after nouns and verbs to show that the person or things mentioned are very much above the average in excellence of parts. The first personal pronoun is divided into three divisions, so that a speaker has the power and great benefit of a large choice in the manner that he might wish to address his listener. Should he be a very eminent personage he can put himself in a high dignified position at once, or should he desire to be lowly the same thing is effected by the mere

choice of the pronoun, or if he be desirous of
flattering the person he addresses that is also easy
of attainment by the same simple process. The
second personal pronoun is even more varied in its
grades of expression than the first, as it is divided
into six parts, not to mention some lesser ones
which may all be employed, should the usual forms
of the pronoun not be found sufficient. Thus in
the mouth of an able student of Burmese it is with
the greatest ease that he can dignify, flatter, snub,
or scold by the mere alteration of the pronoun. So
one is led to imagine that Burmese must be a most
useful language for a nagging wife or a cantanker-
ous husband to employ!

The Burmans also possess many ways of saying
"yes." They can agree with you in a homely
commonplace manner, or they can make their
acquiescence in true lordly fashion all by the
slight change of idiom. Whether they do the
same thing when "no" is in the question, I am
not so sure, but probably they are far too polite
a people even to say that disagreeable word un-
courteously, as manners is one of their strong
points, and verily one of the most useful and
charming of gifts, for there is no truer saying than
"Manners maketh man," though alas! we of the
West in this bustling nineteenth century are fast
entirely forgetting, or laying aside as quite too old
world, the courtly ways of yore, and one greatly

fears that when another fifty years have sped on
their way politeness (anyhow in England) will
have made his bow and likewise have quite departed.

Another very quaint manner of expression in
Burma, and one which must strike a foreigner as
peculiar, is the way that everything is classified,
or a description given of it, such as a hundred
pieces of money, a hundred flat round things ; four
boxes, four square articles; two women, two respectable beings ; two balls, two round things.
Another feature of the language which is worthy
of note is that the meanings of nouns, adjectives,
and verbs are changed by the addition of a prefix
added to the original root, and not by making any
change in the nouns, adjectives, and verbs themselves.

It is curious that the arrangement of the
Burmese language is exactly the reverse of the
English, while in the case of the Shan, Talainy,
and Karenn it is very similar in construction.
Stops and commas do not figure largely in the
language, and it is written from left to right. The
paragraphs are divided by four short lines placed
in a perpendicular position.

In the alphabet the consonants are placed in
separate parts such as gutturals, cerebrals, palatals,
labials, and dentals. Another rather curious thing
is that each letter of the alphabet has a classifica-

tion or description of its form, such as Ka-gyee
and Ka-gway, great Ka and curved Ka or big-
bellied ta, or steep pa, and hump-backed Ba.

With regard to the literature of Burma it is
composed chiefly of sermons and legends of Gautama Buddha, dealing with his many appearances,
also stories of nats-dewahs and fables. I venture
to quote two from Mr. Scott's delightful book, as
they struck me as particularly quaint and curious.
The first reminds one of La Fontaine, and the
second of the dear old fairy story. I also venture
to quote two little sermons of Buddha from General
Fytche's most interesting book, and a few proverbs
from Mr. Gray's " Burmese Proverbs and Maxims."
These will, I think, give some slight idea of
Burmese literature.

Why Ants are Found Everywhere.

All the animals of the forest came to the Lion-
king to pay him homage. The little ant came
with the rest to bow down before the king of
beasts, but the nobleman drove it away with scorn.
When the king of the ants heard of it he was very
angry and sent a worm to creep into the ear of the
lion and torment him. The lion roared aloud with
pain, and all the animals came running from every
side to offer their services and fight the enemy,
wherever or whoever he might be. But none of
them could do any real good. They could not get

at the worm. At last, after many humble em-
bassies, the king of the ants was prevailed upon to
send one of his subjects, who crept into the lion's
ear and pulled out the worm. Since that time
the ants have enjoyed the privilege of living everywhere and in any country, while the other animals
had all of them their special places assigned at the
division of the earth.

The next one is charmingly simple and amusing :—

The Dog, the Cat, and the Ichneumon.

In the time of the Buddha Gawnagohng, four
pupils—a prince, a young noble, a rich man's son,
and a poor man's son—received their education together in the country of Tekkathoh. When they
had finished their course they asked their teacher,
" What was the value of learning ? " The sayah
replied as follows :—Long ago there dwelt in the
land of Gahapatee Waytha four wealthy men who
were great friends, and each sought to further his
friend's plans as much as possible. At last one of
them died and left an only son. The widow said
to him, " My dear son, my husband, your father,
Moung Bah, is dead, and you take his place and
succeed to all the property ; but you are still very
young. It would be well, therefore, if you went to
your father's three friends to acquire learning and

prudence from them." With that she gave him three hundred rupees and sent him off with a company of servants. On the way they met a man leading a dog. "Hallo! you there," said the boy, "will you sell that dog?" "If you want to buy him," replied the stranger, "you must give me a hundred rupees." The youth paid the money and sent the dog back to his mother. She took it for granted that her late husband's three friends had approved of the purchase, and fed the dog and took great care of it. Another day after he had eaten his noontide meal, he met a man carrying a cat, and called out, "I say, you sir, will you sell that cat?" "Yes," said the man, "for a hundred rupees." The money was paid, and the cat sent back to his mother as before. She thought that this cat must have been recommended by the three merchants as a purchase, and took as great care of the cat as of the dog. Another day, after his dinner, he came upon a man with an ichneumon in his arms, and wanted to buy it also. The man agreed to part with it like the others for a hundred rupees. The rich man's son paid the money and sent it back home. The mother, still under the same impression, looked after it as carefully as the dog and the cat. Now the dog and the cat were domestic animals, and she kept them about the house without any concern, but the ichneumon was a wild creature, and she was in such a state about it that she wasted away. One day, when the monk from the monastery came round on his usual alms-begging tour, to receive his dole of rice, he noticed her appearance, and said, "Dear me, my good supportress, how thin you have grown!" The rich man's widow replied, "Yes, the reason is this: I gave my son three hundred rupees, and sent him off to his father's three old friends to learn business habits, and one day he sends me a dog, the next a cat, and then again an ichneumon; and he gave a hundred rupees apiece for them. Now I don't mind about the dog and the cat, for they are house animals, and I get on very well with them, but the ichneumon is a jungle beast, and the mere sight of it frightens me so that my body and limbs and eyes are all pining away." The yahem advised her to turn the creature loose in the jungle. It is wrong to disregard the counsel of one's teachers or one's parents, and so she set the ichneumon free, not, however, without giving it some food well soused in oil to keep it alive till it was able to look out for itself.

When the ichneumon got into the forest he fell a-thinking: "The rich man's son gave a hundred rupees for me, and since I came into his possession I have been well looked after and fed, and better than all I have now got my liberty again. I must repay him the debt of gratitude I owe." Then he found in a pool in the forest a ruby ring, and carried it off to the rich man's son, and said : "This is no common ring, it possesses the power of gratifying every wish of its owner. Put it on your finger, therefore, and be sure you do not allow any one else to wear it." Thereupon he went off to the jungle again. The rich man's son wished, and during the night a great palace with a pya-that rose up before his house. The king of the country, with all his subjects, came to see the sight, and the king gave him his daughter in marriage. Soon after this the princess's spiritual teacher came to see if he could spy out her husband's charm. He looked everywhere, but he could see nothing but the ring. He therefore came to see the princess by herself, when the prince had gone out, and after making a great number of pretty speeches to her, asked if she was sure of her husband's love. "What a stupid question !" she said ; "he is only a rich man's son, and I am the daughter of a king." "Oh, if he is so very fond of you, then, you have probably been allowed to wear his ring," insinuated the pohnna sadaw. "If I have not," returned she, "I would like to know who should." Then the reverend gentleman went away. A day or two afterwards the princess asked her husband to let her put on his ring. He was very fond of her, and so he took it off and let her have it, but told her on no account to show it to any one, but to wear it constantly on her finger. The pohnna came again another day when the rich man's son was out, and began talking in his usual smooth-tongued way. The princess said, "I have got that ring you were speaking about the other day." " Have you," said he, " where is it? " " On my finger," she said, and showed it. He begged her to take it off and let him examine it, and her nurse, who was also present, at last prevailed on her to gratify the sadaw's wishes, and so at last she drew it off and handed it to him. As soon as he got it, he slipped it on his finger, changed himself into a crow, and flew away to the middle of the Thamohddaya Ocean, whither no one could follow him, and there he stayed under a seven-roofed spire.

When her husband came back and heard what the pohnna had done, he said to the princess, " You showed the ring, though I expressly told you not to do so, and now it is in the middle of the great Thamohddaya sea, and we shall never be able to get it back again." He then remained sunk in a deep melancholy. One day a bevy of the daughters of the nat-dewahs came to bathe in a pond grown over with water-lilies, not far from the house where the rich man's son was born. They took off their necklaces and jewellery and laid them down on the bank. The cat found them there, caught them up, and ran off and hid them.

The houri maidens came to the cat and begged her to return their necklaces, saying they were only fit for nat-dewahs, and not for mortal men. The cat replied, " If I do, will you promise to make me a road to the place where the pohnna sadaw is living under his pya-that in the middle of the Thamohddaya sea? That is the only condition on which I will give them back." So the daughters of nats made the road, and the cat crept stealthily along till she reached the spire, where she found the pohnna asleep, with the ring on his finger. She pulled it off and brought it back to her master as a return for his kindness, saying, " You paid a very large sum for me, and have fed and treated me well ever since." The sadaw, for his part, fell into the sea and was drowned, while the rich man's son, having now regained his talisman, had every wish of his heart gratified.

Some time afterwards a band of five hundred robbers came to kill the rich man's son and carry off his ring. The dog saw what their purpose was, and flew straight at the leader of the band, and bit him to death and dropped his body down a well. The other robbers were so frightened that they ran away. Next day the dog said to his master, " I did not get any sleep last night; I had hard work to do," and then he told how the robbers had come to slay his master and pillage the place, and how he had killed their leader, and so frightened the rest away. He finished by saying, "Now I have made some return for your kindness to me. I have been enabled to save your life and property." "Ah!" answered the rich man's son, "everybody called me a fool for giving a hundred rupees for you, who are only an animal; but I owe all my fortune to three animals, each of which I purchased for that sum." Then he went away into the jungle and brought back the ichneumon and kept him in his house.

Now the ichneumon, the dog, and the cat, each of them asserted that he had a right to eat before the other. The ichneumon, because he first gave the ring to his master; the cat, because when the gift was lost she had taken the necklaces of the dewah daughters, and so by getting a road made for her, had recovered the ring and thus restored her master's fortunes; the dog because when five hundred robbers came to strip the rich man's son of what the others had given him, and to take his life, he killed their leader and dropped him into the well, whereupon the rest of the band ran away. "And thus," said the dog, "I am the preserver, not only of our master's property, but also of his life."

At length they agreed to leave the arbitration of their dispute to the decision of the Princess Thoodammasahree, the daughter of King Dammarit, who reigned at Mahdarit, in the kingdom of Kambawsa. She dwelt in the palace of a Tabindeing (the princess who remains single to be married to the next king), and was well versed in the ten laws : (1) to make religious offerings ; (2) to keep the commandments ; (3) to be charitable; (4) to be upright ; (5) to be mild and gentle; (6) not to give way to anger; (7) to be strict in observing all the religious ceremonies; (8) not to oppress any one ; (9) to exercise self-restraint ; (10) not to be familiar with inferiors, and learned in the civil as well as the criminal code. The fame of her wisdom had spread to the eight quarters of the world, so that the most eminent men from every country came to her for judgment.

The three animals, therefore, came before the princess, and the ichneumon opened the case as follows :—" A certain rich man's son paid a hundred rupees for me, fed me, and housed me well, and set me free in the forest. Having regard for his kindnesses, I gave him a ruby ring, by means of which he obtained a palace with a royal spire, which sprang out of the earth ; therefore I am entitled to take precedence and to eat before the dog and the cat." The cat then followed, and recounted how the pohnna had carried off the ring which the ichneumon had given her master, and how she had got it back

19

again, and so had renewed all his fortune. Then the dog stated his case, saying, "When robbers came to take from our master the ring which the ichneumon had given him, and which, when it was lost, was restored to him by the cat, I killed the leader of the band, and then they all fled. Therefore, I preserved not only my master's property, but also his life, and therefore I ought to have precedence over the two." When they had finished their arguments Princess Thoodammasahree pronounced her decision as follows: "The dog, in addition to saving his master's treasures, prolonged his life also, therefore he is entitled to the first place amongst you; but, of a truth, there are none among animals who so well understand how to repay a debt of gratitude as you three do."

Thus ends the story of the dog, the cat, and the ichneumon, from which you may learn, that although man is superior to all animals, yet kindness shown to them will always meet with its reward.

"In one of Buddha sermons he thus accosts a young disciple who had gone astray. 'A man should refrain from the six things that are called ruinous, viz., love of intoxicating liquors; the custom of wandering about the streets; too great passion for dancing; games and spectacles, gambling; frequenting vicious company; and, lastly, slothfulness and negligence in the performance of one's duties. Drunkenness is the cause of the loss of goods and reputation, of quarrels, diseases, immodesty of dress, disregard of honour, and incapacity for learning. Unseasonable wanderings expose a man to great dangers and temptation, and leave his family and possessions unprotected. A passion for games and shows draws a man from his occupations and hinders him from gaining his livelihood. A gambler has no friends. In gaming, success is followed by intrigues and quarrels, loss by bitterness and sorrow of heart, as well as dilapidation of fortune. Finally, frequenting the company of the vicious, idleness, and neglect of one's proper duties, lead to debauchery, deceit, robbery, and all kinds of wickedness.' "

In speaking of false friends, Buddha describes them in the following excellent way :—" As always making show of friendship without its reality, professing a love which they do not feel, giving little that they may receive much, and being friends with a man only because he is rich, or because they have need of his favour. Those, too, are false friends who give a promise in words, but are far from fulfilling it in their actions; and, finally, those who are ever ready to assist a man in doing evil, but never in doing good. Real friends, he adds, are of four kinds : firstly, those who are such both in adversity and prosperity; secondly, those who give good advice on proper occasions, even at the peril of their lives ; thirdly, those who take care of whatever belongs to him they love ; and fourthly, those who teach a man what is good who are delighted in his prosperity, and sorrowful in his misfortunes."

The proverbs quoted have a quaintness about them, and with all some very trite reasoning.

" He is a wise man who looks upon another's wife as he would upon his mother, upon another's property as upon a clod of earth, and upon all creatures as he does upon himself."

" Prolonged is the life of one who eats with his face to the earth; he is wealthy who eats with his face to the south; he is famous who eats with his face to the west ; one should not eat facing the north."

"A man is only half until he finds a wife. A childless house is like a cemetery."

"People see the fault of others, though big as a sesamum seed ; their own, as large as a cocoanut, they do not notice."

"Sleeping late, remaining idle, behaving with severity, sleeping long, travelling alone, paying attention to another's wife—these, indeed, are not for one's advantage, be he even a saint."

" Now it is cold," " now it is hot," " now it is too late." " The moments slip past those who neglect the performance of actions with thoughts such as these."

"One should praise teachers before their face, friends and relatives behind their backs, servants while at work, and sons and wives when carried off by death."

"If a man could catch the air in a net, bale away the ocean with one of his hands, or produce sound too from his own hand, he would then satisfy women; such, verily, is woman's nature."

"They who stand by you in sickness and in adversity, in famine and in captivity, at a king's door or in the charnel-house—they are friends indeed."

CHAPTER XIV.

ONE of the most important events in the life of a Burmese girl is the ceremony of having her ears bored. It comes on the threshold of her womanhood; it is her "coming out," her introduction to society—her entrance into the world.

After the mystic earrings are placed in her ears the maiden begins to look into the future, to dream perchance of lovers and marriage; she takes an interest in a new tamehn, and in the arrangement of the flowers in her hair, and she begins to practise the peculiar swing when she walks that all Burmese belles affect. She will also have her own cheroots, and not be obliged to be satisfied with an occasional whiff from her mother's. The world and all its delights is opening out before her, but before those delights can be secured the great ceremony of the ear-boring has to be gone through.

This ceremony generally takes place at the age

of eleven or twelve. With the Burman's very superstitious nature, the first thing to be ascertained is a lucky day and hour for the ceremony to be performed.

This is attained by inquiring of a soothsayer, and when a fortunate day and hour have been at length decided upon, great preparations are made. A large feast and Pwè are arranged, and all the friends and relations are bidden to attend.

It is looked upon as such an important function that no one likes to refuse without a very serious reason. The company generally arrive in good time, and they arrange themselves round the front portion of the room; in fact, they take the seats from which they can get the best view of the proceedings.

The girl whose ears are about to be bored reclines in the back part of the room, and is generally surrounded by her female relations, who encourage and console her by turns. The girl probably feels much as we do when we go to the dentist. The soothsayer, who on this occasion is mighty in the extreme, walks to and fro with his eyes on some mystical chart; close to him is the professional ear-borer, the man who is to perform the operation. He is armed with gold needles. These needles are nearly always of gold, but never, even in the case of very poor people, of baser metal than silver, and some rich people have been known to have them studded with precious stones. The company remain on tenterhooks of excitement, waiting for the desired sign from the wise man, and the girl becomes every instant more nervous and excited, and at last very nearly works herself into hysterics at the thought of the mystic rites to be performed upon her. At length the soothsayer gives the longed-for signal, and the ear-borer rushes upon his victim and swiftly and deftly passes the needles through the lobe of the ear. The girl generally expostulates vehemently and vociferously, but she is restrained by the women round her, while the music of the Pwè without and the chattering of the company within successfully drowns the girl's piercing cries.

The needles are left in the ears, and are bent round and moved religiously backwards and forwards every day. Should the people be very poor, a piece of string is passed through and kept there instead of the needles. This is moved daily until the wound is healed, after which the important process of enlarging the hole begins, and making it of such dimensions that it is possible to insert the "na doung," which is a gold cylinder measuring about an inch in length, and in diameter about half an inch to three-quarters. The enlarging the hole takes some time, and is effected by sundry methods, none of which are particularly agreeable to the patient. The first method is to pass through the hole a gold plate tightly rolled up ; by degrees the elasticity of the metal tends to expand, and thus it enlarges the aperture. Another method is to insert the stems of elephant grass, adding two or three stems daily until the hole is of sufficient proportion. After this has been done for a certain time an ear-plug, called a "nah-kat," can be inserted. This ear-plug is large at both ends and smaller in the centre. These "nah-kats" are gradually increased in size until the happy, glorious moment arrives when the "na doung" can be worn. The "na doung" are, as I have said, gold cylinders, and set very often at the end with beautiful jewels, emeralds, rubies, and diamonds. In King Thebaw's time there were very strict regulations with regard to the wearing of jewels, and none of the ladies at Court were permitted to wear any jewels unless they had been bestowed upon them by Queen Soo-Paya-Lat herself. Many of these "na doungs" are cut out of amber, but those of the poorer people are generally only coloured glass.

The tattooing in a boy's life holds quite as important a place as the ear-boring in a girl's. He would not consider that he had fully attained to manhood without the mystic characters being depicted upon his body, and he is not satisfied until his body, beginning a little below the waist, and covering his loins and thighs down to the knees, is a mass of quaint devices and beasts, such as tigers, monkeys, elephants, birds, while nats and curious compound animals called tigerbeeboos, are not uncommon. The operation of tattooing is extremely painful, and the boy is usually put under opium during the process. It is generally the custom for only a few figures to be done at a time, as the part swells a great deal, and there is a danger of fever, and the irritation is at times almost intolerable. There have been cases known when the whole surface was finished at one sitting, but that is almost an unheard-of thing.

The instrument used is a pricker, which measures some two feet in length ; this is usually heavy at one end, and it is often decorated by a figure, which, in the case of a good sayah or tattooer, is generally carved. Sometimes it takes the shape of a bird, or a nat, or beeboo. The style portion of the instrument is solid ; the point being sharp, and split into four long slits, which hold the colouring material. The style is about three to four inches long, and fastens into a hollow pipe, which is again joined to the end. In this way sufficient length is attained without too great weight. The manner that the sayah works is by holding the pricker with his right hand and guiding the point with the forefinger and thumb of his left hand. The liquid used is the finest lamp-black that can be produced by the burning of sesamum oil, water being added as it is required. It is a general custom with the best sayahs to sketch the outline of the design first with a paint brush, and the pattern is then manipulated by puncturing on the lines very close together, which produces afterwards the effect of one rough line. Each figure that is tattooed has a framework composed of a tracing of alphabetical letters.

Tattooing is carried to an even greater extent with the Shans than the Burmese. The Shans cover the body from the waist to well below the calf of the leg. The best sayahs are Shans, and they generally carry a little book containing drawings, so that each person may choose his own design. In Rangoon it used to be said that the woman who was tattooed desired an Englishman for a husband.

As I am, alas! drawing near to the end of my little sketch on Burma, I think that I cannot end it more aptly than by placing a description of a Burman's death at the close of this little volume.

When a Burman makes his exit from this world many quaint ceremonies are enacted. As soon as the breath has departed out of the body, and the first grief has subsided, a message is despatched to the Pohn-gyees, who are summoned to attend. The body is placed beside the principal post of the house, the "Thabyay-teing," after which all the friends and neighbours are bidden to come, and a band is stationed without the house and instructed to perform funeral dirges. The corpse is entirely washed, and the two big toes, and sometimes the thumbs, are tied together, if possible, with the hair of a son or daughter. The body is then swathed in a white cotton shroud, after which the best tamehn, or pasoh, that the corpse possesses is put on. In the case of rich people this is often very magnificent. The face is nearly always left uncovered. Between the teeth they place a piece of money, which is supposed to pay for the soul's passage across the mystic river, which the Burmans firmly believe to exist. In the case of very poor people a betel-nut is often the only toll put between the teeth.

The band, should there be one, continues to play dirges outside the house, but as the band is looked upon with disfavour by many of the monks, its presence is often dispensed with. It is usually the custom for a few Pohn-gyees to remain in the house near to the corpse, so that their presence may scare away any evil spirits. The coffin is the next thing which is thought of, and that is generally not of very solid construction. It is usually made of let pan (Bombax Malabaricum), which is a thin light wood of the same nature as deal. This is fastened in a very rough way with anything that may be handy.

The friends and relations come and offer their sympathy, and tender their aid in decorating the bier and hearse, many of them bringing money and food. The Burmans are most willing to help each other, and generosity is usually a very strong characteristic of theirs, and is one of the tenets laid down by Buddha.

In the case of a death, especially in Lower Burma, the friends bring rice, fruit, betel nut, and some fabric for beautifying the bier, which often enables a poor man to have quite a grand funeral.

The length of time that the corpse is kept depends entirely upon the status in society that a man occupies. Should he be possessed of riches his funeral arrangements take some time to prepare. While if he is poor, he is interred with all speed.

The rich man's funeral ceremonials last as long as his relations think fitting to his dignity, and as long as any money remains.

It is almost a matter of necessity that all blood relations should attend. The coffin, or "hkoung," is adorned with the dearly loved tinsel, coloured paper, and gilding; the "talah," or bier, has a light canopy in the shape of a spire, and is carried by means of bamboo poles. The decoration of this spire is generally most florid and glaring, pasteboard, tinsel and painting, playing a large part in the ornamentation. It is usually manufactured in

the street in front of the house, for it often rises
to an enormous height, some twenty or thirty feet.

On the day of the funeral a goodly company of
Pohn-gyees arrive, and there is a sermon given,
dealing with the vanity of human wishes and
desires, and the changefulness and uncertainty of
life upon earth. After which dissertation the
coffin is brought out and deposited upon the Talah.
As a kind of pall, there is generally thrown over
the coffin either a tamehn or pasoh. Occasionally
the coffin is gilded and made very ornate with
figures of lions, tigers, and elephants, in which
case the garment of the deceased is looped up so
as to display the beauty of the coffin. At length a
long procession is formed, which accompanies the
bier. First come the alms intended for the poor
and the monks ; these are borne by persons of both
sexes. After the alms come the Pohn-gyees, and
after them comes a band of music, and sometimes
a troupe of singers. In very close proximity to
the band is the coffin, borne by six or eight young
men, while clustering round are a large number of
friends and relations of the deceased. Now and
again the bearers of the bier stop and dance a
strange slow measure to the dirges performed by
the band, and songs are occasionally composed by
an improvisatore, which deal with life and death,
and eulogize the departed one. It is occasionally
the custom to have a tug of war at the grave, like

what is enacted at a Pohn-gyee Byan, one side crying, " We must bury our dead," and the other saying, " You shall not take our friend from us." The former are always victorious, but they have often to enlist recruits from the crowd around to aid them in their efforts. It was, and I believe still is, a matter of faith, that a funeral should not go in a northward or eastward direction. The graveyards usually lie to the west.

At Mandalay, in King Thebaw's time, the dead were only permitted to be carried out of the city by one especial gate.

When the grave is at length reached, only the intimate friends and chief mourners remain while the last rites are performed, the rest of the company betake themselves to one of the zayats (or rest-houses), of which there are always many in the vicinity of the graveyard. Here they are entertained by the refreshments dear to a Burman, cheroots, sweet drinks, betel, &c.

On the arrival of the coffin at the grave the band stops playing, and the alms are given to the Pohn-gyees, who recite the five secular command-ments, and the ten good works, &c.; after this short service is finished, they also depart. The chief mourner then pours a little water out of a cocoa-nut shell, making use of words to the effect that the departed one and all present should share in the merit obtained from the almsgiving. The

idea of this is that the earth shall bear witness.
" Shway Yoe " gives the following legend concerning it :

" When Shin Gautamo ascended the throne under
the bawdee tree, Mahn-nat the devil claimed that
it was his, because he had discovered it first, and
all the mighty host shouted aloud when he called
upon them as witnesses. The Lord Buddha had
no witness but the Earth, and to it he appealed,
asking whether he had not achieved the three
Great Works of Perfection, the Ten Great Virtues,
and the Five Renouncements ; the Earth gave
testimony to this Koung-kmoo with a terrible
roaring and a violent earthquake, so that Mahn-
nat and all his legions fled in terror." This is the
reason for the pouring out of water when alms are
presented.

After that ceremony, the coffin is swung three
times backwards and forwards over the grave and
then lowered slowly down. This performance is
called "oo-teik-thee," and is intended for a last
farewell. Each person also throws a handful of
earth into the grave, and the coffin is then
covered.

For seven days subsequent to the funeral the
mourning continues. In the case of a rich man
this mourning means endless feasting; it is, in
fact, a kind of prolonged wake. Streams of
visitors arrive professedly to offer their con-

dolences, but possibly the chance of a good dinner may influence, and materially increase, their sorrow for the deceased. The Pohn-gyees also come and receive offerings, and friends kindly bring contributions to help in the expense, but even then the cost is great of maintaining this hospitality, and it oftentimes falls very heavily upon the heir, who finds that his patrimony has sadly dwindled in that one riotous week of feasting. Even in the case of poor people this feasting is generally done in a minor degree, and is often a very heavy tax upon them.

In old days, burning was the most general way of disposing of the dead, and is still practised to a certain extent in the jungle districts, but now burial is gaining in popularity and is almost invariably practised in all the British possessions.

I have endeavoured to place this very slight sketch of Burma and the Burmese before my readers, with the hope that it may awaken in some, and increase in others, an interest in this charming country, which has, up till lately, been little known among English travellers. It is a country which possesses an infinite charm and attractiveness—an attractiveness which has not as yet been quite ruined, nor has its primitiveness been utterly destroyed, by contamination with our European civilisation !

For those who desire to make a journey which will take them rather further afield than the usual Indian tour, and who are interested in seeing our latest possessions in the East (not counting the sterile hills round Chitral), there cannot be found a more delightful tour than that up the Irrawaddy. As you glide along in the luxurious Flotilla Company's steamer you have presented to your gaze the most picturesque scenery, the most fascinating inhabitants, and some of the wildest country that is to be found in the East; add to this (in the winter months) a charming climate, and I think that you will agree with me that few things in life can offer more seductions than a journey in Burma.

Our last week there came to us with a great and sincere regret, and we felt a real melancholy creeping over our spirits as the days fled away and the hours that we were to spend in that delightful country became less and less. There is a subtle charm and attraction in Burma which it is difficult to describe, or lay fully before those who have never been there. To those who have either visited the country, or who have lived there, even though the latter may have certain faults to find and many drawbacks to recount, still, I think they will allow and agree with me that there is an indescribable something about Burma, the people, and the life, that seem to wind curious tendrils of affection about one's heart and make the leaving of it a real pain.

We spent our last week at Rangoon under
the hospitable roof of our ever-kind friends,
Mr. and Mrs. Donald Smeaton. The heat was
too great to allow of our going out much
after ten or eleven o'clock in the morning till
half-past four o'clock in the afternoon, when it
became quite delicious, a cool balmy breeze
springing up which just stirred the trees, and
seemed to bring refreshment with every breath
—refreshment after the long blazing, panting
afternoon which we had spent, reposing in as airy
attire as it was possible, and either reading or
thinking with our eyes shut, until lengthening
shadows or the cooling air warned us that the
great and mighty sun-god was at last taking his
adieux for that day and going to leave us to enjoy
the little daylight that remained. Those gloaming
hours were spent in lovely, dreamy drives along
the shores of the lake in the Dalhousie Park, the
ponies' nimble little feet ringing out a soft accom-
paniment to our talk, while the delicate reflections
of the trees threw darkening shadows on the water,
and the Great Pagoda loomed out of the gathering
gloom like a mighty shrouded figure that seemed
to grow and take a majestic grandeur upon itself
in the half-fading light. As I gazed on its
glorious proportions, four other monuments would
rise also before my eyes. Each in its way had
cast a spell upon me, and would always inspire

me with the same lingering friendship, the same
longing to return and behold it again in sunshine
and in rain, at early dawn or dewy eve; each
would always appear to me as a friend. The four
others were St. Mark's at Venice, the Duomo at
Sienna, St. Peter's, and the Taj—a curious company, three Christian churches, one Buddhist
temple, and a Mahometan tomb; and yet there
seemed some strange affinity among them, and
each in its way would woo me to return and
behold it again; and would seem to tell me in its
own romantic language that it gave me a true
and ready welcome back.

Our last evening came, and we spent it in the
charming square porch-like verandah with the
punka flapping slowly backwards and forwards,
backwards and forwards, making a kind of rhyth-
mic, somniferous sound as it cleaved the air with
clock-like precision and sent a faint breeze around
us which kept away that arch-fiend, the mosquito,
who was, however, ever ready to pounce down upon
any nice fresh morsel of flesh that presented itself.
We did not find the mosquito quite as irritating
and tiresome a personage as his character had led
us to suppose; but he certainly was at his worst
upon the Irrawaddy, especially upon the lower
part of the river, and there he played round and
hummed and buzzed in one's cabin till I longed to
be able, had it been possible, to have slaughtered

his father and mother, brothers and sisters, ancestors and descendants, and thus happily to have exterminated the whole detestable species.

There are all sorts of ridiculous stories told of the mosquito in Burma. A common one related to unsuspecting foreigners is that in one place they are so well grown that they have been shot for snipe. One might be led to wonder if the imagination of such gallant sportsmen had not been a little aided by, let us say, Scotch whiskey! Certain it is, however, and absolutely true, that in some parts of Lower Burma the ponies sleep under mosquito curtains, otherwise they would be driven wild, poor little beasts, by the bites of these venemous creatures.

The mosquito always seemed to wait for the happy moment when one was comfortably settled down to write a letter. He would then begin his attacks, at first mildly and almost courteously, then more persistently and a little rudely, and lastly so viciously that you would get wild with indignation and fling paper, pen, and probably ink, if it was not all dried up, in the air, at the offending monster; and yet, in spite of mosquitoes, earthquakes, and heat, my heart felt very sad on that last evening at Rangoon, and still heavier the last morning when, at six o'clock, we bade farewell to our kind friends and found ourselves driving down to the quay, along the wide roads shaded

with arching boughs of trees, whose lovely green
foliage had not yet been quite tarnished by the
dust. We took a last farewell look at the lovely
groups of little Burmese ladies, all looking so fresh
and sweet on their way to market.

Arrived at the quay, everything was of course
screaming confusion, and, what was worse, we

SHIPPING AT RANGOON.

found that the ship that was to have taken us
to Madras had broken down, and that a horrid
little boat rejoicing in the name of the *Kishna* was
to take her place. The ship was crowded with
natives of India who lay so thick upon the deck
that you saw nothing but a confused seething
mass of humanity which was neither pleasant to
be near nor to look upon. We took also as many

European passengers as was possible, and thus the very small deck accommodation left to us was also crowded.

Deck chairs jostled each other in such close proximity that it was difficult to find even a corner free for one. After the usual bustle and flurry and leave-takings, some tears and some smiles, the ship was at length cast off from the quay, and we began to drift slowly down the river. It was no easy matter to thread our way between the crowd of craft of every description from a man-of-war to a native dugout which jostled and crowded up to Rangoon ; but by degrees we passed out and away from this large fleet, and left the noise and the rush behind us, and steamed away between green banks. Rangoon was left like a faint mirage in the distance, and nothing but rice mills again obtruded themselves upon our gaze. Now and again we caught a glistening picture of the great and glorious pagoda standing out in its superb majesty from the low green hill, but at each turn of the river this picture grew less and less distinct until it looked like a great golden tear hanging from the sky.

As I stood with my eyes fixed tenderly upon it, a lady said softly beside me, "I have lived for twenty years in Burma, and now I am leaving it for ever, and going home for good; but somehow I cannot bear to take a last farewell of the Great Pagoda, which I have gazed upon for so many years that it has become like a dear friend."

I turned and watched her go silently below, and then turned my own eyes seawards. Somehow a mist seemed to gather before me and blur the glistening speck, and a feeling of melancholy possessed me with the thought that I, too, had probably paid a last farewell to that golden shrine. I leant silently on the taffrail, watching the white foam that the screw made, curling and swirling itself into soft white bubbles.

Were the last weeks a charming fantastic dream, or had we really made one of the most delightful journeys that this Old World can still offer?

FINIS.

UNWIN BROTHERS, THE GRESHAM PRESS, WOKING AND LONDON.